THE BOOK OF OWLS

LEWIS WAYNE WALKER

THE
BOOK
OF
OWLS

 ALFRED A. KNOPF NEW YORK 1974

THIS IS A BORZOI BOOK
PUBLISHED BY ALFRED A. KNOPF, INC.

Library of Congress Cataloging in Publication Data

Walker, Lewis Wayne.
  The book of owls.

  1. Owls. 2. Birds—North America. 1. Title.
QL696.S8W26   598.9′7′097   73–20746
ISBN 0–394–49218–8

Manufactured in the United States of America

First Edition

CONTENTS

ACKNOWLEDGMENTS

Much of the factual material in the following chapters I wrote either as scientific notes or popular articles that appeared in the following magazines or journals: *Boys' Life*, *Animal Life* (Canada), *Animal Life* (England), *Nature Magazine*, *Reader's Digest*, *Natural History Magazine*, *National Geographic*, *Life*, *Look*, *Arizona Highways*, *Audubon Magazine*, *The Auk*, *The Condor*, *Time*, *Newsweek*, and others.

Factual material, in most cases credited in the text, has also been gleaned from *The Auk*; *The Condor*; Albert K. Fisher's *Hawks and Owls of the United States*; John and Frank Craighead's *Hawks, Owls and Wildlife*; Arthur A. Allen's *Stalking Birds with Color Camera*; *Birds of Arizona*, by Joe Marshall, Allan Phillips, and Gale Monson; Casey A. Wood's *Fundus Oculi of Birds*; *Birds of Prey of the World*, by Shelly and Mary Louise Grossman and John Hamlet; and *The World of the Great Horned Owl*, by G. Ronald Austing and John B. Holt, Jr.

FOREWORD

LEWIS WAYNE WALKER
December 12, 1905–June 4, 1971

Lewis Wayne Walker was a field naturalist and ornithologist and natural history interpreter who lived to explore the natural world and to share his discoveries with any who would look or listen. With his photographs, writings, and museum displays he told about what he saw. Because he understood and loved nature sooner than other men he was a conservationist long before it was popular. Nearly half a century ago he wrote of the economic value of predatory animals—hawks and owls and coyotes and mountain lions—and pointed out the fallacy of so-called predator control.

Lew Walker was a born naturalist. As a child he haunted the woods and fields and marshes near his home on Long Island Sound. As a young man he apprenticed under the great Carl Akeley in the preparation department of the American Museum of Natural History. And as a young man he spent ninety-six nights in the bell tower of the First Congregational Church in Flushing, Long Island, studying and photographing a pair of Barn Owls nesting there, and learning that they brought 758 rats and mice to feed their chicks. This study marked the beginning of Lew's long interest in owls.

Lew Walker went to Colorado, and then to San Diego and the Natural History Museum there, to prepare some of the finest bird dioramas of the time, and while in San Diego he developed a great interest in Baja California. In World War II he enlisted in the Marines and wrote a book, *Survival Lore*, to save pilots' lives. It included his desert ecology observations, which recently appeared in his popular book *Survival Under the Sun*.

After the war Lew returned to San Diego and his explorations of islands off Baja California and of the Sonoran Desert. In 1954 he was called to the new Arizona-Sonora Desert Museum, where he was associate director. The exhibits of that unique institution reflect his genius for nature interpretation. He and his wife, Melanie, retired in 1970 to a retreat near Julian, California, to devote time to research and writing. It was a great misfortune that his time was so short. He died on June 4, 1971.

Lew Walker wrote more than two thousand popular articles and scientific papers during his lifetime, and he made great contributions to natural science. Probably the one that gave him greatest personal satisfaction was the preservation of the endangered nesting populations of Heermann's Gulls and Elegant Terns of Raza Island in the Gulf of California. For this he enlisted the interest and financial support of his able and interested friends. And of course he had the cooperation of other friends, distinguished ornithologists and photographers, in the preparation of this book about owls—which itself is one of Lewis Wayne Walker's major contributions to natural history.

GEORGE E. LINDSAY
Director
California Academy of Sciences

PREFACE

An explosive screech from a darkened sky made me pause on my way to the train station at Flushing, Long Island. The time was about 9:30 p.m. in February 1926. On the left were the railroad tracks that carried commuters from suburban homes to offices in the largest city in the world, its center only a few miles away. On the right were the typical rural structures of the day, stores, houses, apartments, and in their midst a frame church with a bell tower high above the other buildings. As I stared into the night, city lights suddenly reflected off the white underside of a flying bird that eerily circled once and then disappeared into the belfry.

This sight was reported at the next scout troop meeting, which was attended by Daniel Carter Beard, founder of the scouting movement in the United States and a long-time resident of the community. My report kindled his memories, and if he had a prepared speech on general scouting it was entirely forgotten. For the next hour the troop was spellbound by his accounts of owls in the same church, first brought to his attention forty-six years before. At that time there were two churches situated several blocks from each other and the congregation of one of these was often disturbed by rasping hisses from the bell tower above. In an effort to quiet this noise an owl was occasionally shot, but despite these presumably spasmodic deaths the remaining mate always showed up the following year with another, thus forming a chain of many links, which maintained the nest for almost half a century. During this same period the birds were also forced to vacate periodically when chickenwire was erected to block their entrance. They would then take up their abode in the other steeple several blocks away until the ravages of weather reopened their chosen home.

A few days after Dan Beard's talk I met the sexton of the church and received his okay to make a quick trip to the top of the tower while he waited below. After endless steps I raised the trap door and was deluged by a cloud of debris, forty-six years of accumulated refuse from foods the owls had brought in. The floor was covered with a black powdery dust to a depth of about half a foot and every few inches over the entire expanse the bleached white skulls of rodents could be seen. Underneath a favorite perch was a heap of fresh pellets, the indigestible parts (fur and some bones) coughed up by owls a few hours after a meal. I scooped some of these into a small box and then left the tower. These strange objects, refuse to most people, were treasures to me.

For the next week I spent every spare minute poring over pellets, dissecting fur from bones, and stacking skulls to one side for future identification by the helpful mammalogists of the American Museum of Natural History. And a week after classification had been determined I inveigled an invitation to a meeting of the powers that ran the church when the so-called filthy owls were not only on the agenda but also were making themselves heard by the staid audience below. As the birds continued to call, Dan Beard and I looked at each other and by some mental telepathy knew that our cause as saviors of the most beneficial birds in the world hung by a mighty thin thread. The vibration of one or more screeches echoing first in the belfry, then from wall to wall in the tower, and finally from pew to pew could have broken that thread when we were called upon to present our case.

Strange sermons have been delivered in churches, but never one so imbued with the common sense of natural history as that made by Dan Beard. His only props were two museum mouse skins and a blackboard. With the rodents representing an Adam and Eve of their species, and his skilled hands drawing pictures and family trees, he captivated the small group, stressing the need for those predatory checks now so well recognized. As his chalk lines created pre-Disney caricatures of Mickey Mouse it became plain to all that any offspring of his Adam and Eve could breed at the tender age of six weeks, that each pairing would produce from four to six young in a litter, that there would be from six to eight litters a year, that at the end of a very few seasons the world, Flushing in particular, would be crawling with vermin if the owls were not permitted to live and do their work. To illustrate pyramiding numbers the daily doublings of monies with a one-penny starting deposit were drawn on the blackboard. This gave a pocketbook flavor to his dissertation and was followed with Darwin's famous quote—daring, considering the day and the surroundings: "Lighten any check, mitigate the destruction ever so little, and the number of the species will almost instantly increase to almost any amount."

My exhibit, the hundred pellets removed from the belfry a week earlier, now had a semblance of order. A compressed pile of fur was held down by a net on one side of a three-by-three board, and radiating from it were the labeled skulls of rodents the fur had concealed while in pellet form. The array was astounding, even though it represented no more than a fifty-day catch for the two birds, which were periodically interrupting the meeting with their explosive voices. A blasé reporter of a local paper, indifferent up till this point, took notes as I reeled off the catches made by the owls: 122 field mice, 86 Norway rats, 19 house mice, 3 shrews, 1 weasel, and 1 bird. A doctor in the group suggested trading cats for owls and another man wanted to borrow a bird for just one night to put in his basement. On adjournment there was no doubt that a reprieve for the Barn Owls had been earned. With the belfry key in my pocket I was launched on a career delving into the night life of birds that even now are still surrounded by mystery.

THE BOOK OF OWLS

Disturbed Barn Owl "toe-dusting"

1

BARN OWLS

On a cold, dreary March day I lifted the trap door and saw, in one corner of the belfry, an egg with two owls perched on a rafter above it. The birds nervously glanced back and forth as though to take flight and then began to dust their talons with their chins. This, as I learned later, was characteristic of owls when disturbed, and despite our association during the next three months their reaction when I appeared was invariable. With wings half spread and feet wide apart they started this slow and brushing swinging motion. The activity lasted a minute or more before a slight easing in motion could be detected; then two long faces appeared from beneath the lowered bodies. Brown eyes, seemingly black against the white heart-shaped facial disks, stared at me, and the toe-dusting actions continued.

Picture yourself as a small predatory animal of skunk or raccoon size. Next look into a hollow tree, an old mine shaft, or an erosion hole in a sandbank, sites used by Barn Owls for nests the world over. The light is dim, or possibly the night is very dark, when suddenly a ghostly white object stands out from the black. It is at least three feet across, a foot in height, swaying, pivoting, and ready to pounce. As you try to make a decision on your next action, the cavity you were about to enter echoes with a series of sharp snapping noises as though dry twigs were being methodically broken. This is followed by a noise like a steam jet being opened, slowly at first and then wide to a gasping crescendo.

There is no doubt that this ferocious-looking pose and the shrill accompanying sound effects have worked well through the ages. If not, Barn Owls in their varied forms would not have a worldwide distribution, excelled by few other birds. In reality Barn Owls' bodies are deceptively small, roughly about the size of a closed fist, but their long legs developed into the world's most efficient rodent traps and their large wings give a false sense of size.

When clicking mandibles, gasping screams, partly spread wings, and toe-dusting failed to make me leave the belfry on that first visit, both birds vacated by flying through the skylight. Had they known that in the following days I would average at least four hours of observation a night in all probability they wouldn't have returned. Lying beside the single egg that was white and almost round were three field mice and one Norway rat. The first day of a ninety-six-day study was over.

The next night there were eight rodent carcasses piled around the lonely egg, and in the tabulations of subsequent months I found that this was close to the average nightly catch. However, nightly catches varied sharply and before long it was apparent that weather was a controlling factor, but just how or why remained a mystery at that time.

The whole problem of correlation of food and weather is intriguing. In the ninety-six consecutive nights applied to the study, or from the time the first egg was laid until the last young one left the nest, my mildewed notebook shows that the owls brought in 758 rodents and 1 bird. The greatest catch on any one night was 27 rodents, with the smallest catch just a single rat. But a final perusal of the same figures disclosed a pattern, a gradual build-up to a dozen carcasses in one case, and once to over two dozen. These periods of abundance were followed by sudden drops, as though the owls' hunting ability had been severed with a knife. After my observations were completed and I was attempting to extract reason from chaos, someone suggested weather reports. At once the pattern was clear. During days of relative dryness and lowering humidity, the catches climbed, but even a meager rain would send them crashing to the low-number bracket. Days were required to build back to a peak.

Thus the "why" was explained, but the "how" still remains a mystery, not only for the Barn Owls of this initial study but also for other species of owls that I have studied through the years since.

Take four plausible theories about the effect of weather on owls' hunting. First, presume that rodents stay hidden during rainy periods. This sounds logical and is logical while a storm is in progress, but the high percentage of field mice caught by the Flushing owls, and the high percentage of pocket gophers caught by California Barn Owls subsequently observed, must be taken into consideration. Both field mice and gophers live in underground burrows, usually in porous soil and often in depressions where even a slight rain makes home remodeling necessary. Then they must come to the surface, while at other times they can subsist on underground roots or on previously stored food that is completely out of sight of flying predators.

The second presumption is that the owls do not hunt during inclement weather. From my observations I know this is true. Owls often sit out a storm in some protected spot, and inactivity would of course make that night's catch unproductive. But my catch tabulations showed a slow build-up to a peak through periods of many rainless days after a storm, days (or nights) when the owls were definitely hunting but with rather mediocre results.

Third, there is the possibility that moisture cancels the ability for silent flight. On the main flight feathers of all owls the forward edges of the quills are lined with soft barbules that permit them to fly very quietly. This feature is not as well developed on the diurnal Pygmy and Burrowing Owls, or on the arachnid- and insect-eating Elf Owls. But Barn Owls are masters of this art of noiseless approach. If the feathers were wet or even damp the benefits of this quilled padding would be negated, but here, as with the rodents, the gradual rise to a peak after a single rain must be taken into consideration. I failed to see how a slight variation in humidity could have such a drastic effect on hunting prowess by warning the prey before the owl could strike.

The fourth possibility, based on the sound-deadening effect of damp foliage, formerly had loopholes as unreasonable as those listed above. A few years ago, however, some revealing experiments by Roger Payne of Cornell University showed that owls have supersensitive hearing. It was found that Barn Owls, once accustomed to a room and deprived of all light, could, if a mouse were let loose, pinpoint the sound of the animal and make successful catches. However, it is only natural to suppose that a dampened footing for the mouse would have a soundproofing effect that would partially negate the wondrous hearing of the hunting owl. This discovery tends to clear up the mystery of the weather's bearing on the nightly catch, which had me baffled for several decades. It also explains the extremely large ear openings that all owls have.

I return to my initial study. That first egg laid remained solitary for three days. Then a second was deposited, followed two days later by a third. Incubation began between the laying of the second and third eggs, but for the next eight nights additional eggs were laid, until the total clutch numbered eleven.

Aside from a scooped-out hollow in the debris that covered the floor there was no attempt at nest building, but if, during incubation, a feather or any other prominent object appeared within reach the setting adult would often tuck it under her feathers. This spasmodic arrangement gave a semblance of a ring around the eggs, which evidently satisfied a latent instinct for nest building.

The setting pose even on this flat floor was grotesque to say the least. The primaries of the long wings were laid parallel to the ground and the wrist was thrown far forward. From this pose the famed swivel neck worked to perfection, allowing the incubating bird to scan all three hundred and sixty degrees.

During the egg laying and for a short period thereafter both birds occasionally left the belfry together. While flying close together they would utter a peculiar rapid clicking noise that was definitely vocal and not made by snapping bills. In the few instances where observations were possible, copulation usually followed a landing after these flights. Later in the season, when young were being fed, these calls were almost never uttered and did not resume until a second clutch for the year was about to be laid.

The most common call heard was a penetrating rasping, hissing screech audible for at least a quarter of a mile. This seems to have at least two uses, both warning in nature. On the relatively few occasions when my presence in the belfry surprised the owls, they in turn surprised me with this hair-raising screech as they flew out the open skylight. Its explosive quality would no doubt stop a hungry predator momentarily, allowing the birds time enough to make a getaway.

During the feeding of the young, the adults, both singly and as a pair, did most of their hunting in an area used as a city dump—later part of the site of the 1940 World's

Fair. When a single hunter returned from these forays the screech would be uttered about every ten seconds, and even though traffic noises and perhaps distance alone kept it from my ears, the sudden attention of the nest-guarding parent gave a clue that it had been uttered.

The hunting range of the Flushing Barn Owls seemed to have been roughly limited to four miles, but that was possibly controlled by the overabundance of rodents that normally inhabit every city dump; or, in short, why shop all over town when there is a supermarket on the corner? On the deserts of Arizona and the plains of Colorado I have heard and seen Barn Owls foraging for food at least ten miles from the nearest nesting or roosting spot. Circumstantial evidence based on pellet findings in the Coronado Islands shows that these island birds make repeated trips of about ten miles over water, and possibly through fog, which often covers the southern California and Mexican coastlines in May and June.

Just above the landing on the northernmost island of this group there is a sheer cliff with numerous crevices and caves. From one of these I retrieved a bushel basket of pellets, believing that these insular residents, where the only rodents known were deer mice, might have placed birds on their menu. When the pellets were examined, however, the results showed that the owls were flying to the mainland and bringing back pack rats and gophers. These two rodents, unknown to the islands, were so common in the pellets that the trips had to be of almost nightly occurrence.

The first two eggs laid at the Flushing nest hatched on the same day, followed by the next nine on succeeding days. The incubation period was thirty-three days. This presented a peculiar nest of young, with the last to hatch ten days younger and considerably smaller than the first two, which had emerged almost simultaneously. The early uncontested eating by the oldest fledglings had developed them rapidly, and within a few days after all the eggs had hatched it was obvious that the youngest three or four had only an outside chance of surviving. Their feeble movements could not compete with the vigorous actions of the others in begging food from the adults. The axiom "Might makes right," especially in filling a stomach, widened the gaps in size each day.

These infant young also had to be fed tiny bits of food from the beak of a parent, but the older ones could pick up a small mouse and swallow it with ease. Whenever idle and not sleeping the latter would search the floor with their beaks and seize any-

thing soft. On one of my trips through the trap door I caught a glimpse of a leg of the youngest owlet disappearing into the gullet of the oldest. This cannibalism continued spasmodically until only seven of the original eleven remained. I don't think real hunger caused this devouring of younger brothers or sisters. If it had been, some of the disappearances would have occurred during or after a rain, when the catches of the adults were so meager that the entire family subsisted on a starvation diet.

At an age of three or four weeks the fledglings developed efficiency in a running walk, balanced on both sides by trailing wings. This new-found mobility dispersed the huddled mass of young to corners and crannies all over the belfry. I also noticed that at about this time the owlets began to recognize the distant screech of a returning parent. If hungry, they would respond by leaving their corners and huddling in the depression that had been the nest, and the screech always stepped up the tempo of the hiss with which they seemed to indicate hunger. This noise, somewhat similar to the sh-h-h-h used by humans to request quiet, was uttered by the young within a few days after emerging from the eggs. As they grew in size it mounted in intensity and just prior to flying was audible for several hundred feet.

Bill clicking when disturbed seems to be a characteristic of all owls. Adults are usually so skilled in making this noise that the mechanics producing the sound are not visible, but the owlets' inept attempts to snap their bills make the whole procedure one of slow motion. By careful observation one can see the following steps: the bill opens, the tongue protrudes on one side or the other, the bill closes, the tongue is withdrawn, and the bill under pressure snaps together. Adults can perform this feat in a different manner with such rapidity that the clicks are heard in a continuous chain. The procedure used by the inexperienced young is probably painful, for if they are forced to do it repeatedly the tongue coating is scraped off and copious bleeding results.

At an age of about six weeks the young began to develop their wings, exercising them by flapping continuously and raising clouds of dust. At seven weeks they could lift themselves off the floor and occasionally were able to alight on rafters, their favorite targets. The early evening visits of the parents changed when the two eldest showed a proficiency in the air. Instead of dropping through the skylight and proffering food the adults now perched on its edge with a rodent dangling from their beaks. This tantalized the offspring to greater heights and at just eight weeks of age one of the two that were first hatched managed to hit the edge of the skylight and struggle to the

Four-week-old Barn Owl

roof. A few hours later I could hear his rasping hiss of hunger from a flat-roofed apartment several hundred feet away. The next night he was back in the belfry, having successfully completed his first solo.

Malnutrition of the youngest of the seven surviving offspring showed as tiny whitish lines on primary and tail feathers, and although the first five left the belfry in perfect shape, the last two incurred broken wing feathers at points where the hunger streaks showed. That development had been retarded was also evident by their first outside flight: both were at least one day over the age standard of forty-nine days set by the others when they first flew outside.

Ninety-six nights after the first egg was laid the last of the young left the belfry, and I left too, thinking my owl study was over. Three days later, however, I received a call from the sexton reporting a little pile of rats and mice stacked at the edge of a roadside drain. From far below street level a rasping hunger call had been stopping pedestrians and drawing the anxious adult owls into making momentary rodent delivery stops whenever the curb was clear.

That evening, feeling foolish, the sexton and I went to work, but the storm grate covering the owl's tomb was unyielding. A passerby facetiously suggested a wad of gum on the end of a stick and if it had been quarters being retrieved that would have been the solution. But this owl, young in age, seemed old in experience and either nimbly stepped out of rope loops or grabbed them with his talons so they would not close.

By midnight fatigue forced us to call the street department, and within minutes the crew lifted a manhole cover twenty feet away and pointed to a ladder that dropped to a dark passageway. As I crawled on hands and knees to corner the bird in a bend, he uttered terrific screeches that echoed and vibrated around and around, coming out blocks away.

These bizarre underground noises precipitated numerous phone calls, and as I ascended to the street with the bird clutched in my hand, still screeching, sirens could be heard approaching from all directions. When second-story windows opened on nearby dwellings I had a hunch that any further work on Flushing's Barn Owls would be anticlimactic.

According to rumors the owls nested in the belfry for two years thereafter, but I kept away from the area, slept at night, and allowed them to live a well-earned peaceful existence, for this study—publicized at the time it was made—helped to bring nationwide protection for this beneficial species. However, this same publicity, which eventually saved thousands of owls by separating fact from fancy in regard to diet, caused the demise of the Flushing pair. Several years after concluding my work on the birds, I found their lifeless forms in a museum cabinet. According to the label attached to their legs, the collector was an ornithologist who, as a guest, visited the belfry during my study.

MEASUREMENTS   Length 14–20 inches; wingspread 45 inches.

VOICE   A sucking intake of air, as though a person were impolitely slurping soup, is the note used by the Barn Owl young when hungry. This call is often uttered by only one of a nestful of fledglings and when the caller ceases to utter it is taken up by a brother or sister. Early in the evening it is repeated every few seconds but after hunger is assuaged it sometimes becomes spaced to a half minute or more. It is normally heard only after dark and is first apparent when the young are about four days old. At that age, however, it is so weak that it carries only a few yards. With increase in size it increases in volume and just before an owl's first flight carries for several hundred feet. After leaving the nest the flying young continue to utter the call as long as they are dependent on the adults, which is usually from six weeks to two months.

If Screech Owls had this next call, or if Barn Owls bore the name of this smaller, eared cousin, common names would have some meaning, but usage makes such a transposition impossible. In other words, the screechingest nocturnal bird is the Barn Owl, and the whistlingest is the Screech Owl. The screech uttered by Barn Owls is explosive, and aside from its short duration it might be compared to a pre-diesel locomotive letting off steam. It seems to have three meanings, two of these signaling alarm, one for the bird and one for the luckless person or small creature that gets close enough to warrant it. Its third use is open to conjecture. When a Barn Owl is flying high in the air, completely undisturbed, it will often utter this call every half minute or so and with such volume that it may be heard for a half mile or more. At the Flushing nest the fledgling owls often aroused from slumber minutes before my ears detected the screech of an adult as it approached the nest. Possibly it's a vocal signal of location which works like the visual rump patch of antelope, or the scent sign left on low branches by traveling peccaries.

Another note is seemingly used when a pair of Barn Owls are flying in close proximity, consisting of a series of metallic-sounding clicks. I have never heard this uttered by a single bird, and since a few times after such a clicking flight copulation followed, it might have some connection with courtship.

NESTING   Barn Owls are not at all particular in their choice of home sites. In the old days crevices in cliffs, holes in sandbanks, and hollow trees were no doubt their top selections, and all of these situations still meet with favor. Now, however, buildings such as churches, granaries, or dilapidated barns add a new type of shelter, resulting in the accepted common name of the species. Barn Owls have also been found on ledges, deep down on the vertical walls of mine shafts, within the brown skirt-like leaves of California's Washingtonia palms, and in underground burrows dug originally by badgers or coyotes, and even on the exposed platform nests of hawks, ravens, or crows. In open country each pair seems to control three or four square miles of territory but in some areas where suitable home sites are scarce I have found at least four pairs occupying a quarter mile of pock-marked cliff.

The number of eggs contained in a clutch varies almost as much as nesting sites. Some pairs that have returned to the same nest year after year seem content with three or four, while others habitually lay as high as eleven.

Although this may be a hasty conclusion, some "birth control" seems evident, based not on the number of offspring a pair can adequately care for but based on the nest area their future young will cover. In my experience, those pairs nesting in the confinement of hollow trees, in space seemingly far too small to accommodate even one adult, are usually satisfied with three or four eggs. Those nesting on roomy platforms of barns or silos, however, often double and sometimes almost triple that number of offspring. The eggs, averaging 43.1 × 33 mm, are dead-white in color and ovate in shape (they are not as round as most owl eggs). In the southern part of their range Barn Owls have been found nesting throughout every month of the year, and some pairs, to my own knowledge, raise at least two and possibly three broods a year. In northern areas one brood seems to be customary.

A pair of young Barn Owls in a tree nest

HOURS OF ACTIVITY   Although there have been a few records of

Barn Owls hunting on cloudy afternoons, I have found them to be strictly nocturnal even though their eyesight in daylight is excellent. One that I liberated flew from my hand for a block or more close to the ground and then rose steeply, looking directly into the sun, and landed on a telephone wire. There was certainly nothing blind about that bird, or for that matter any other owls I've observed in similar daylight flights.

FOOD   Any creature continuously referred to as "the most beneficial bird in

the world" has had to earn that reputation; until a few years ago the owl was labeled a "varmint," and considered better dead than alive. Unfortunately, there are still small but vociferous enclaves of ignorance that fight the facts, on owls as well as other birds of prey and animal predators.

The facts below are not based on the aesthetic qualities of Barn Owls, even though they are one of the most beautifully plumaged birds in the world. Compassion for a misunderstood creature also has no bearing. Instead, in the case of Barn Owls the facts can be interpreted in terms of actual cash value, a language all of us understand. This cash value prompted William Leon Dawson, author of *Birds of California*, to write: "In its destruction of pocket gophers alone a single barn owl is worth from twenty to fifty dollars per annum to the State of California. When to this is added its services in destroying meadow mice of the *Microtus* group, the bird's economic value is beyond calculation." The quotation above was probably inspired by the reports of competent authorities that ground squirrels and gophers annually destroy ten percent of each year's crops in California. This destruction has at times been so great that ranchers, townships, and even counties have occasionally paid bounties of ten cents a head on gophers. It's too bad that Barn Owls can t collect their share of these monies and hire lobbyists to fight those people or organizations wanting open seasons on practically everything alive. That the owls' share would be tremendous is intimated by the great naturalist William L. Finley when he wrote: "An old owl will capture as much or more food than a dozen cats in a night. The owlets are always hungry; they will eat their own weight in food every night and more if they could get it. A case is on record where a half grown owl was given all the mice it could eat. It swallowed eight in rapid succession. The ninth followed all but the tail which for some time hung out of the bird's

Barn Owl with a just-captured meadow mouse

*Full-grown Barn Owl
returning home with prey*

mouth. The rapid digestion of the Raptores is shown by the fact that in three hours the little glutton was ready for a second meal and swallowed four additional mice."

In general I believe every field naturalist in our country champions Barn Owls, but that there are deviates among these birds, just as there are in the human race, has been demonstrated several times. Paul Bonnot, working the coast of California, writes: "There was an old cabin on the Island which had fallen partly to ruin. Under a built-in wooden bedstead was the nest of a Barn Owl. The area covered by the bed was three inches deep with feathers, wings and bodies of Beal Leach Petrels. These little birds were evidently so easily caught that there were numbers of bodies with only the heads removed."

Bird-eating by Barn Owls probably occurs because of geographical limitations, such as a rodent-free island. Personally I loathe hot Mexican food but will eat it if nothing else is available, and while eating Mexican food on Cardonosa Island in the Gulf of California I found nesting Barn Owls that had also been forced to change their diet. The nest was on the upper edge of a rock crevice that tapered downward like an ice cream cone. Remains of Least Petrels, fish bats, and some Craveri's Murrelets filled this funnel to a depth of three feet. I couldn t determine the horizontal depth into the cliff, but it seemed to be in excess of several yards and it was packed tight with the accumulation of years of these unusual foods.

That Barn Owls occasionally make mistakes of identification and catch birds instead of rodents seems evident from a food report by Dr. Charles W. Townsend. He reports that 56 pellets found in an attic of a rice mill near Charleston, South Carolina, contained the remains of the following mammals and birds: 2 small shrews, 65 rice rats, 1 cotton rat, 7 Red-winged Blackbirds, 12 Sora Rails, and 4 Clapper Rails. He also notes comments by A. K. Fisher on the unusually high percentage of birds: "I am wondering whether rails and other birds that in a way simulate the movements of rats and mice in the thick foliage might not be taken by accident rather than intentionally by the owls. This theory would seem to have some weight because they do not molest pigeons that are breeding in adjoining apartments or any species that are not found on the ground around marshes or fields."

The explanation sounds plausible, especially when I remember a study I made on a pair of Barn Owls nesting in a pigeon loft that was filled with "White Kings," a distinctive variety of poultry that could not possibly be mistaken for anything else. The location was a service building, complete with attic, in the center of a square of primate cages in the San Diego Zoo. The top floor was devoted to the raising of "White Kings," which flew about beautifying the garden. One spring, Barn Owls took up residence in this dovecote and although Mrs. Belle Benchley, then the director, didn't necessarily distrust their motives, she called me in to check on their menu.

The room was small, about ten by twenty feet, and thirty or forty pigeon nests were scattered about the floor while some were in boxes nailed to the wall. A few had eggs and others young in various stages of growth, while over in one corner young Barn Owls swung their heads back and forth at my intrusion. Within two yards of this meat-eating family, pigeons were sitting on eggs or brooding their tasty squabs. With this tempting culinary thought in mind I watched the predatory birds for many nights, checking on the foods the adults brought their young, and I came up with the following figures: 52 rodents (rats, gophers, and mice) and 1 shrew. Examination of a number of pellets showed a preponderance of rodent skulls and also the remains of three (young?) pigeons. It may well be that these three birds succumbed during the moving-in operation, particularly if they had occupied a space coveted by the owls. Even though I expected the observations to absolve these birds of prey, the sight of pigeons by the dozens clustered around the owls was incongruous. It was a scene that would not have been believed several decades ago, when owls were almost universally on the unprotected list, placed there on hearsay and not by fact.

So far I have centered on the unusual and even touched a little on the rare deviations from the normal. To get a correct aspect of the latter, A. K. Fisher's monumental work *Hawks and Owls of the United States* lists the following: 703 pellets from Dr. Bernhard Altum (locality of collecting unknown) contained 16 bats, 3 rats, 930 mice, 1,579 shrews, 1 mole, 19 English Sparrows, and 3 other birds. Two hundred pellets from Washington, D.C., contained 225 meadow mice, 2 pine mice, 179 house mice, 20 rats, 6 jumping mice, 20 shrews, 1 star-nosed mole, and 1 Vesper Sparrow. Four pellets from Greensboro, Alabama, contained nothing but the remains of cotton rats. Also from A. K. Fisher are the following statistics on the stomach contents of 39 Barn Owls collected from Maryland to California: 1 contained poultry (a pigeon), 3 contained other birds (Cowbird, finch, sparrow, and towhee), 17 contained mice, 17 held other mammals, 4 held insects, 7 were empty.

There are the food statistics on America's most beneficial bird, made by competent observers, but just what has the research meant apropos of a sane conservation program? A few protective laws have been put on the books, but stiff convictions for killing Barn Owls are scandalously rare. Ask any game warden about the number of suspended sentences that result from prosecutions for the slaughter of owls or hawks. In time even the minions of the law get discouraged.

OF SPECIAL INTEREST   It is interesting to note that some islands in the Pacific are benefitting from American Barn Owl research. One of these, Lord Howe Island, several hundred miles off the coast of Australia, formerly owed its economic independence to palm trees. These plants were raised by the thousands, shipped all over the world, and were much in demand because of their ability to thrive in the darkened lobbies of hotels and waiting rooms. But several decades ago a few chicken breeders commenced to lose newly hatched chicks and blamed their losses on owls native to the island.

On a comparatively small Pacific island it was easy to wage a war of extermination, and within a few months the upsetting of natural balance commenced to be felt. Rats, the real culprits in the chicken killing, increased alarmingly and began girdling the small palms until that export industry almost became a business of the past. In desperation island authorities appealed to the British government, to the U.S. government, and finally to the San Diego Zoo, in an effort to mend the catastrophe that the unwarranted slaughter of owls had created. Young Barn Owls were collected from all over San Diego County and shipped to Lord Howe Island. From latest reports their reintroduction has remedied the situation.

Another somewhat similar situation occurred in the Hawaiian Islands. There are seven main islands in this chain and on four of these mongoose were introduced in an effort to check the population of non-native rats that were accidentally introduced. On islands where the mongoose reside, the super-destructive ground-loving Norway rats are in the minority, kept in partial check by these controversial mammals, but on the other islands the Norway rat, without any check, causes costly damage to the plantations. Some years ago the Department of Agriculture and Forestry, loath to introduce mongoose to the other three islands, approved the introduction of Barn Owls. Eighty or ninety of the birds were liberated, and according to Paul Breese, former Honolulu Zoo director, they were subsequently seen catching and eating rats.

2

SCREECH OWLS

Desert heat, northern cold, eastern humidity, or Death Valley dryness are one and the same to the large group of Screech Owls, whose individuals are capable of establishing year-round homes in almost any environment. These, the smallest ear-tufted members of the nocturnal owls, are probably the most common of all, and seemingly exist wherever the cavities in plant growth afford them daytime seclusion. In my experience it is only on the grass-covered plains of the west that they are entirely missing.

Such adaptability combined with a sedentary nonmigratory nature has permitted genes of inherited characteristics to run rampant along narrow lines. Throughout the ages natural barriers such as mountain range, valley, river or gulf have enforced isolation, limiting genetic dilution to a degree impossible to a more freely wandering species. As a result the scientific "splitters" have had a picnic in the naming of subspecies. At some later date many of these will be questioned by the "lumpers" and relegated to oblivion. Some are sufficiently different to be readily recognized. Others fool even the experts. But despite these differences, largely based on minor characteristics, there are some Screech Owls differentiated well enough to warrant a subspecific name.

The race inhabiting the eastern states is the largest of the wide-ranging group, but their main claim to fame is their occurrence in two color phases, red and gray, colors that are not due to age, sex, or season. In most areas these colors are about evenly balanced, and the pairings of the adults will be mixed and only by chance mated according to color.

A study made in 1893 by E. M. Hasbrouck claims that gray Screech Owls were the ancestral stock and that from them came the reds and intermediate phases. It is also stated that the offspring of reds, or a red and a gray, may be all red, all gray, or of both colors, but that there is no record showing the offspring of a pair of grays to be anything but gray.

I have a very strong recollection that when I was a boy there were areas on Long Island and in upper New York State, Massachusetts, and Maine where one color or the other held a dominant position. In fact I firmly believe that if these woodlands are still in existence I could pretty well predict which color would most likely be encountered and I would probably be right nine times out of ten. At the time I don't believe I wondered why, but—and this is more recollection—as I look back on those rambles there were sumacs, oaks, and maples—foliage that attains a seasonal redness where most of the red-phase birds were found. And where the grays were most often encountered I seem to remember extensive forests of beech, ash, and black walnut. Could this be evidence of a trend toward protective coloration? In time will color separate the two phases where color has a survival value?

While on the subject of red- and gray-phase Screech Owls, a general note in the April 1954 issue of *The Auk* by A. W. Schorger is of interest. Over a period of eighteen years Schorger made 639 trips between Madison, Wisconsin, and Freeport, Illinois, a distance of seventy miles, and examined 235 Screech Owls killed by cars. Gray-phase birds predominated, with 61.3 percent of the total, while red-phase were far less so, 38.7 percent. In the same general note he mentions that in 1891 C. F. Carr published a note in *The Wisconsin Naturalist* stating that he had handled over twenty-five specimens of Screech Owls and had never seen a gray-phase. Does this mean that a radical change has occurred, since the gray-phase now predominates about two to one? It is clear only that the color-phase issue is as yet unsolved.

Screech Owls are birds that are small in stature but large in heart. To appreciate their prowess one should make some comparisons concerning the relative strength of owls in general, based on the creatures they capture. Barn, Long-eared, and Short-eared Owls rarely attempt to capture prey larger than Norway rats, yet Screech Owls, which are only about half the size of the cousins mentioned, tackle and subdue these rodents whenever presented with the opportunity. Their carrying abilities also stretch far beyond what one would imagine for their stature. On numerous occasions I have found prey in Screech Owl nests that weighed approximately as much as the bird that carried it home. But despite their laudable prowess, they are retiring creatures rarely found in the open, and they are quick to drop into a hole if disturbed when sunning at the entrance. They are also extremely nocturnal and from my experiences seldom permit undue familiarity from the human race.

When I once found a nest twelve feet from the ground in the knothole cavity of a sizable oak, I carefully considered these secretive characteristics of Screech Owls. Would the birds tolerate a structure that housed not only a human but also cameras, storage batteries, and reflectors? The structure was bound to be large and I wondered what construction technique would be least likely to cause desertion. Some birds can stand a sudden shock and then quiet down in a few hours, but the same birds may become increasingly nervous and finally desert if disturbance is carried on intermittently over a prolonged period of time. Other species, upon seeing a large box on four legs close to their home, are liable to panic and flee immediately. I finally decided on intermittent disturbance. On the first day I planned to set up the legs, top them with a platform, measure flashbulb reflector distances, and then leave hoping for the best.

Darkness was imminent before the reflectors were in position and luckily I decided to make test exposures at the site instead of at home. The cameras were barely ready when a single low-pitched whistle broke the stillness. Rigid and in plain view on the platform, I heard the call answered from within the tree cavity. Then, as I watched, the opening became blocked; the movement was barely discernible. This slow motion stopped when a wide owl's head gazed in wonderment at the changes made while she had been incubating eggs.

A press on the camera release bathed the area with an instantaneous light from three flashbulbs. When my eyes once more became accustomed to the darkness I glanced toward the nest hole, which now seemed to be plugged with oak-patterned bark. Then as I strained even more I saw that this bark pattern was formed of eyes closed to mere slits, ear tufts raised to jagged points, facial feathers vertically aligned simulating bark furrows to perfection. This ten-second change from wide-eyed curios-

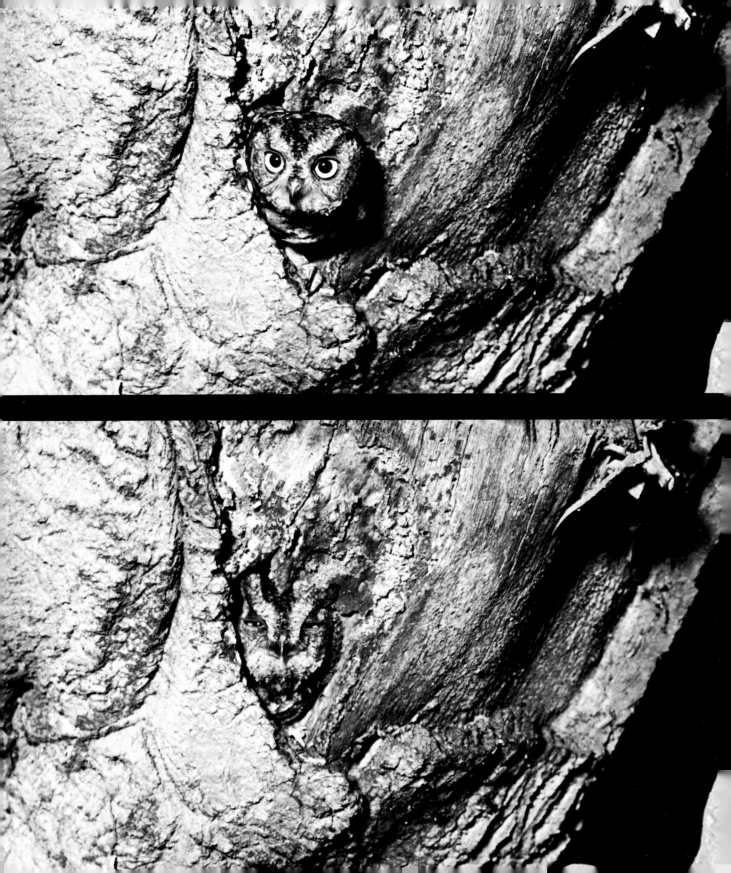

ity to the ultimate in protective coloration and form by the simple use of a few muscles was a truly astounding performance.

The next day, after finding the owl brooding and none the worse for her sudden fright, I again went to work on the blind. By late afternoon it was a boxlike structure completely hiding me and several cameras from outside view, but just why such a contraption didn't defeat the purpose for which it was intended has never failed to mystify me. Here it was, a large incongruous box bigger than a refrigerator, lifted eight feet off the ground on four-by-four stilts. On its front were shiny reflectors and, between them, openings for cameras and eye slots to aid my observation. Camouflage was entirely omitted, for in years of photographing other birds I had come to the conclusion that most species are never fooled. Leafy branches soon wither and droop and the green cloths used in jungle warfare invariably wave in the breeze and instead of helping have a scaring effect. A simple rigid construction that neither groans nor creaks seems to alleviate fear in the shortest time, even though its artificial appearance is completely foreign to the wild surroundings.

I waited three days and nights before I thought the birds could tolerate more disturbance. During this time some, if not all, of the six eggs had hatched, as evidenced by the faint rasping calls of hunger emanating from the cavity when darkness fell.

Within minutes of the same degree of darkness that had induced the adult to show her face several days before, the opening became blotted out again, but this time it was the bark pattern that appeared and not the countenance of wide-eyed wonderment. For ten or fifteen minutes we had a staring contest — the owl from the hole in the tree and I from between the narrow slots cut in the plywood. Just when I believed that my rigid pose must be changed, that my seat should be higher and pillow-padded, that the slot should be larger, and that Novocaine should be a "must" to relieve the cramped muscles of bird photographers, the owl's eyes opened wide and she launched from the hole and disappeared in the darkness. My tension did not ease, however, for within seconds of her flight another face plugged the opening and when it seemed that I must shift position a single low whistle from the first bird induced the second to join her. This was the only time during the entire study that I saw both adults in the hole at the same time.

From then until about ten thirty the nest hole was a busy portal. During the two or two and a half hours the adults carried in four Jerusalem crickets, several grass-

A Screech Owl vanishes: two pictures, taken only ten seconds apart, show a Screech Owl literally disappearing into the woodwork as it assumes a protective posture

hoppers, one woodrat, two pocket mice, and two deer mice. The visits made with insects were hurried to the point of the adult going in loaded and almost instantly reappearing, but those made with rodents entailed longer stays. Later, after folding up my equipment for the night, I climbed to the nest hole and reached in. I could feel the just-hatched young in a slight depression surrounded by the carcasses of that night's rodent catch. As I brought out the carcasses I found that each had been neatly decapitated. The only head remains I was able to recover, entirely by feel, had the brain cavity exposed and were picked clean. Such operations necessary for the feeding of the young probably explain the long stays when rodents were delivered.

The same general pattern of behavior followed the next night, but dusk and the call of an owl in the woods nearby showed that only one adult had attended the young throughout the day. A frog and a small snake were added to the regular nightly foods, along with a few small moths. By late evening the nest with its floor space of slightly less than a square foot must have been pretty well stocked with provisions, and several minutes after the female delivered a pocket mouse she reappeared at the entrance with the beheaded carcass. Switching it from beak to feet in flight and then back to beak again, she alighted on a branch and then unhurriedly surveyed the surroundings with the rodent remains held in her talons.

During this momentary pause her mate returned, saw the rodent on the bough, and gently removed it from her grasp. He flew to the nest with it in his bill. This move produced a peculiar reaction from the female Screech Owl. As her mate disappeared within the trunk she ruffled her feathers, snapped her beak a few times, and flew to a perch within a few inches of the cavity. The moment her mate ventured forth she dived within and came out with a beheaded carcass, which she proceeded to swallow whole in a series of jerking gulps. Facetiously, this might have been her way to forestall an impending family argument, but in all probability the initial removal was motivated by personal hunger and not by a desire for a less cluttered house.

In the remaining nights of observation I never saw another carcass removed from the nest, so I presume that meals taken by the adults within the tree kept the nest from overflowing. At this time the young were covered with a sparse gray down and their eyes were closed; they remained closed for almost two weeks. As the infants grew in size and strength, so would their appetites, hence an oversupply of foods was really only a temporary problem.

Screech Owl delivers a meal
to its young inside nest

Returning to the blind night after night, tabulating foods, calls, and behavior, I suddenly became aware that there had been a gradual but definite change of diet. On the first night of observation I had seen rodents, a few beetles, but no moths. On the second night there was a snake, a frog, rodents, and several moths, and on each night thereafter the larger prey became increasingly scarce while moths of many species were brought in almost as fast as the birds could leave and return. Such diet changes were unheard of in such a short space of time, but there was no mistaking my notes. And then a faint shadow passed over the oak. An instant later another moth was delivered, then another shadow and another moth. Fascinated, I almost detected a rhythm.

Then I remembered the tiny light, powered by a storage battery, that I had installed twenty feet behind the blind to give me vision on the darkest nights. Squirming around in the cramped quarters I finally located a crack that permitted me to see the glowing bulb. One of the owls was standing within inches of the tiny reflector, and while I watched, the bird reached down, picked up an insect, and flew to the nest. As it left the electrically equipped box, its mate took its place. For the next half hour they shuttled back and forth, these nocturnal opportunists that were letting the advantages of the electrical age overpower an ancient, instinctive fear of brightness.

Food statistics on these Screech Owls after the first few nights began to look like those on nighthawks or Whip-poor-wills and were worthless, so I put an amber filter over the light. This retarded the phototropic urge of the insects that previously made it a veritable death ray, and the owls were once again forced to work for a living.

On several occasions something in the darkness far beyond the range of my vision caused both owls to become exceptionally alert. Once they even flew off uttering their questioning whistled "whoo" and for several minutes thereafter I could hear their snapping beaks. The sounds came from an area about fifty feet wide, and from the changing positions of the mandible clicking I surmised that the birds were in constant zooming flight. Two nights later the animal that probably had caused these disturbances came into sight.

With the light now filtered the owls had gone back to their original routine, which meant extended stays away from the nest in search of food. On one of the return trips, burdened with a deer mouse, the female flew as usual right toward the nest opening, but suddenly veered away and landed on a branch, dropping the mouse; she didn't even watch it fall to the ground. Instead, her interest seemed focused on the back of the nesting oak and with fast-turning head she almost tried to see around both sides of the massive trunk at once.

Her gaze pinpointed a spot just outside my line of vision. For a moment there was a churring note interspersed with rapid beak snapping. Then she spread her wings and dived to attack the white-furred snout of an opossum just poking around the tree. With her rounded quail-like wings she reached maximum speed in the several feet separating her from this enemy, and with dragging talons she raked the intruder along the length of his body. This swift attack took place despite a veritable maze of oak branches that should have impeded her progress.

The first onslaught was so precipitous, and vicious, that the mammal's hold was almost dislodged, but now warned of impending danger he ducked lower and forged toward the nest hole like an invincible slow-moving tank. Repeated dives by the owl, now aided by her mate, failed to stop the opossum's progress and this left me in a quandary. Death, like life, is normal with all living things, and, theoretically at least, a life history study should not play favorites or permit human participation to interfere with the normal. If this had been a house cat, scourge of our native birds because evolution has not yet developed a protection from this introduced creature, I wouldn't have hesitated. Suddenly, however, the status of the opossum dawned on me. This animal, too, had been foolishly introduced to the west and like most of the misplaced exotics was wreaking havoc as a foreigner in a previously balanced land.

Practically falling out of the blind I rushed to the tree just as the opossum was attempting to push his head into the nest hole. As I reached for his furless prehensile tail, which curled about my hand on contact, a dive from one of the enraged owls drew blood from my forehead. Retreating, I was forced to duck continually and as I bobbed along, the age-old assertion that there is never any thanks for interference in a family fight passed through my mind.

When the young were a little over a month old, both adults found outside roosts and left their fledglings unattended during daylight hours. At about five or six weeks of age the eldest of the youngsters began to peer out of the hole soon after dark, and this venturesome young one, monopolizing the entrance, received most of the food as it was delivered. Pangs of hunger forced his brothers and sisters to compete, and there were often two heads wedged in a space large enough for only one. This pushing and

Opossum on a raiding mission

pulling for control eventually squeezed a young one out of the hole and on weak wings he successfully navigated a few feet of space and clung to a twig.

Throughout this study the owls showed their disapproval of my presence by occasionally snapping their bills as I entered or left the blind. But it was all bluff and no action until I had interfered in their feud with the opossum. With one of the fledglings exposed to danger, however, the situation changed. Parental protective action rose to a feverish pitch, and throughout the rest of the study the statement that they were even-tempered—all bad—would aptly describe their state of mind. A moment after my foot searched the darkness for a ladder rung the talons of a fast-flying bird sliced through the skin of my ankles. My car, parked several hundred feet away, was a welcome haven reached after a fast run spurred to top speed by the alternating attacks of both adults.

Strange things are done for glory, science, or call it what you choose. The morning after the young owl had left the nest, I talked Pat Kirkpatrick, an expert with an electronic flash, into an evening with Screech Owls. Cameras, reflectors, and batteries were set in position at a spot about midway between two of the owls' favorite perches, which were fifty feet apart and about thirty feet above ground in adjoining sycamores. This arrangement gave the owls every break but supplied absolutely no cover for Kirk or myself, and before that evening was over the protection of umbrellas, crash helmets, or medieval armor would have been welcomed by both of us.

My first battle baptism of the night occurred when I balanced on a ladder with my arm in the hole up to my elbow, searching the interior for the largest of the young. He found me at about the same time I found him and we both grabbed, but his sharp claws pierced the sensitive tendon that connects thumb to forefinger. There I was, hanging well above the ground in the proverbial closed-fist monkey trap! As I attempted to inch the bird toward the opening where the talons could be disconnected, the enraged adults were methodically slashing one side of my head and then the other.

Walking back to the camera set with a whimpering young one was another ordeal I will long remember. It was as though the adults were on long pendulums that swung in a half circle. The two highest points were thirty feet or so above the ground and the lowest point was my uncovered head. If I turned to face an attacking bird, to

Multiple-exposure photograph shows adult Screech Owl attacking the author. Fledgling clings to his hat

ward off a scratching blow, it would zoom harmlessly by while the mate, out of view, would put its talons to work. Their strategy was perfect and executed almost as though it had been rehearsed many times. It is possible, however, that this trait of attacking from the blind side had been acquired from song birds and other diurnal birds that harass owls in the same way if found in an unprotected situation.

Such complete exposure was mine in a very few moments. As Kirk called directions — "A little to the right," "Back to the left," "Stand up," "Stop ducking" — the pair of owls were executing a pinwheel flight. As long as the fledgling in my hand remained calm the blows on my head were light, but if he fluttered or uttered a call the tempo of the hit-and-fly attacks became frenzied; the talons cut deeply. In desperation I clamped a hat on my head but this did not baffle them at all. Only one set of talons scraped its surface and from then on they reached under the brim as they whizzed by, shredding unprotected ears instead of areas that until a few moments before had been partially cushioned with hair.

Kirk was having a picnic, changing films and pressing releases as fast as his hands could work. Each time I tentatively asked: "Think we have enough?" his answer would be: "Lots more film." "This is wonderful." "Stick it out a little longer." And then a reprieve came in an unexpected way, as the fledgling owl fluttered from my hand and came to rest in the heavy grasses under a camera tripod. From then on the attacks that had been aimed at me shifted to the photographer, and within a very few minutes both of us agreed it was time to leave.

Later, after some seventy-odd photographs had been developed, they were laid out on a large illuminated ground-glass table. Those of the actual strike were placed in a vertical line down the middle, those of the approach to the right, and those of the attack-finish to the left. Similarity of wing positions at any specified distance from my head was immediately apparent and some of the negatives of each vertical line could be stacked one on top of the other with hardly a feather misplaced to alter the over-all alignments.

A few nights later, when I was once again able to run a comb through my hair without feeling too much discomfort, I visited the oak nest again. But the owls had not forgotten that they had been victorious. That one night, when by valiant effort they had driven humans from the area, seemingly made them think they were invincible. And with the young scattered into trees several hundred feet apart, the traversing of

Almost invisible, Screech Owl perches outside nest

trails was a hazardous venture that invited silent attacks from the darkness. After being hit a few more times I began to consider their invincibility and the more I ducked the more I believed that it was a good time to terminate my work on these Screech Owls. There was no doubt that the owls felt that way too.

FLAMMULATED SCREECH OWL

This small owl with very short ears, which is rare to the point of being legendary, differs greatly from most of the birds that bear the name Screech Owl. It is the only one that has brown eyes and unfeathered toes, as well as the only one of the group known to be migratory. Very little is known of its foods. The few stomach examinations that have been made point to insects and arachnids as the chief items. Roger Tory Peterson gives its call as "a mellow hoot (or hoot-hoot), low in pitch for so small an owl; repeated steadily at intervals of two or three seconds."

MEASUREMENTS   Length 7–10 inches; wingspread 21 inches.

VOICE

With the score of Screech Owl races that inhabit the United States it is only logical to believe that there have been changes in the development of the localized forms, in the voices as well as plumage. But in a very general way most of the birds are so closely related that it takes an expert and comparison of tape recordings to detect the vocal differences. First let's discuss the so-called screech from which the birds have gained their name. Is it mythical or is it real? Or is it a call used so rarely, say once in a lifetime, that thousands of competent observers have never heard it uttered? I do not know, and were it not for the fact that Edward Forbush and a few other top naturalists claim to have heard it, I would be adamant in saying that Screech Owls never screech. I have observed these owls in all sections of North America—from arid desert to tropical rain forests, from northern Maine to southern Sonora, Mexico. I have put them to every possible test, have witnessed all their moods both in the wild and as captives, and I've never heard them.

The call most often heard is aptly described by Roger Tory Peterson as "a series of hollow whistles on one pitch, separated at first, but running into a tremolo (rhythm of a small ball bouncing to a standstill)." Most of the western Screech Owls voice this call on an even pitch, but the pitch of the eastern Screech Owl descends as the tempo of the notes increases. In close proximity to a nest I have often heard a "questioning" call that, though lower on the scale, is similar to the first syllable of a teenaged "wolf whistle." If they are excited, as when the pair attacked me and the opossum, a short single bark like that of an excited puppy is occasionally heard. A scratchy whimpering sometimes occurs when food is traded between the parents, and this call is also sometimes voiced from a nest when food is delivered. Fledgling young being removed from a nest voice protest with a similar call. Short, unconnected whistles are also a part of an adult Screech Owl's repertoire.

NESTING   Any nest of a Screech Owl not situated in the hollow of a tree or something similar would be exceptional. The entrances to such homes can be natural, such as those often found in apple trees or in oaks or sycamores. Holes drilled by the larger woodpeckers are used as found, and there is some evidence that Screech Owls will enlarge the deserted homes of Ladder-backed, Downy, and Gila Woodpeckers to fit their needs. They take readily to nest boxes, and are often enticed by these into towns or cities.

Their eggs, like those of all North American owls, are white, and clutches number from four to seven. There are so many localized forms of Screech Owls that a single egg measurement cannot be used to cover them all. Here are a few: Bendire's Screech Owl 1.40 × 1.17 inches, Kennicott's Screech Owl 1.43 × 1.30, Mexican Screech Owl 1.30 × 1.10. In my experience the various subspecies seem to have only one brood of young in a season.

HOURS OF ACTIVITY   In general the Screech Owls are very nocturnal, spending the daylight hours in tree cavities or other secluded spots and not venturing forth until dusk has changed to night. However, during incubation or when caring for newly hatched young a parent bird removed from the nest and liberated will often return to the nest in full daylight. One of Dr. Arthur Allen's protégés made an interesting count of the number of nocturnal food deliveries made by a pair of eastern Screech Owls, based on observations on seven successive nights, starting soon after dark and generally terminating just before dawn. Feeding visits varied considerably in number—as with Barn Owls—possibly because of weather conditions. The average number of visits per night with food was 46, with a low of 14 and a high of 75.

FOOD   In comparing these small predators to the size of the prey they some-times tackle, it becomes apparent that Screech Owls are mighty hunters and almost anything they can subdue may be found on their menu. A. K. Fisher's examination of 255 stomachs of Screech Owls that were collected revealed that 1 contained poultry; 38, other birds; 91, mice; 11, other mammals; 2, lizards; 4, batrachians; 1, fish; 100, insects; 5, spiders; 9, crawfish; 2, scorpions; 2, earthworms; 7, miscellaneous; and 43, empty. Among the mammals listed above were pack rats, flying squirrels, and chipmunks, any one of which could have outweighed the owl that subdued it.

Although insects and rodents are the preferred foods of Screech Owls, there are occasions when circumstance changes their diet to creatures we wish to protect. This is especially true in some of the small bird sanctuaries that have been established across the country in habitats chosen because they have a special abundance of vari-ous kinds of birds. These sanctuaries usually add to an already swollen bird popu-lation by the placing of inviting nest boxes and the planting of foliage that supplies abundant food. Confronted with such an oasis of plenty, the Screech Owls commence reducing the numbers of small avian inhabitants to what might be considered a nor-mal population.

Horned Owl

3

HORNED OWLS

As far back as I can remember, the challenging yet somewhat mournful "whoooo, -who, -who" of Horned Owls has been a familiar sound. The birds exist almost everywhere in the country, and careful listening showed them to be present in almost every wooded area I visited. As a result of their easy availability I passed them by, missing marvelous opportunities to photograph these early-nesting birds incubating eggs set in rings of snow, on picturesque cliffs, in stick nests in saguaro cacti, and even partially underground in horizontal mine shafts.

This "mañana complex" with regard to common birds is not a fault exclusively mine, and it was amply shown a few years ago when a call was broadcast for a good photo of an English Sparrow. Shots of Whooping Cranes, California Condors, and other rarities were readily available but the director of one of the world's largest photo services was stumped by an order for a portrait of the numerous English Sparrows. Until a photographer was especially assigned to do the job, photos of this ubiquitous bird were unavailable, and as far as my file was concerned, constant familiarity with the powerful Horned Owls put them in the same class as English Sparrows. I had practically nothing on their lives or habits. And then a report of an albinistic Red-tailed Hawk carrying nesting material led me into a three-year cycle that took me through three species of diurnal birds of prey, enabled me to witness the formation of a Blue Heron rookery, and produced a study of Horned Owls. It all happened in such a way that I was compelled to make that owl study.

The reported hawk nest was in the center of a grove of towering eucalyptus trees, planted years before by a railroad company under the mistaken belief that the lumber would be suitable for railroad ties. From the venture, southern California's Rancho Santa Fe not only received its name but also became a forested area that drew birds as though it was magnetized. Investigation of the white-feathered hawk disclosed a nest so high on a straight-trunked tree that construction of a photographic blind was almost an impossibility. Although I glanced at the nest periodically during the ensuing season, any thought of a structure for real observation had been virtually eliminated by my first view.

The next spring a walk under the nest precipitated the angry cackle of a Cooper's Hawk, and as I paused, the bird, with bullet speed, hurtled from some nearby branches and dived at the nesting platform. There it was met by a Red-shouldered Hawk that had evidently been incubating eggs in the usurped nest. Right from the battle's start it was plain to see that the latter was no match for its agile attacker, and although the two combatants separated upon hitting the ground, it was the Cooper's that regained the nest edge. For minutes thereafter this bird watched the defeated buteo as it crouched under a bush on the ground below.

Another spring, another bird, but this time the creature that glanced down from its standing position on the nest was a Great Blue Heron and on branches within a fifty-foot radius perched a half dozen others, nervously ready for instant flight. Within a few weeks many of the crotches circling the pioneer nest had sticks wedged wherever the pull of gravity could be thwarted. This sudden establishment of a rookery changed my views on the building of a photographic blind; it wasn't that the work would be any easier, but the labor and danger of placing a structure eighty-seven feet above the ground now seemed worth the effort.

With the departure of young herons in late summer, work on the blind began and progressed rapidly until a height of about forty feet was attained. Each foot upward, however, brought about a narrowing of girth and when the twelve-inch thickness existing at ground level tapered to eight about halfway up, winds did enter the picture. The slightest breeze on the leafy foliage above would swing a clinging treeclimber in a

Horned Owl launching into flight

four- to six-foot arc. Frankly, I didn't like to look down and I hated to look up, because, at destination far above, the thickness of the supporting treetrunk shrank to a mere four inches. But guy wires, combined with persistence and luck, finally brought me to the planned vantage point, where I constructed a blind of sorts.

During the fall and winter, while I waited for the return of the herons, I occasionally showed visiting ornithologists this treetop monstrosity, and their main concern centered on whether or not the contraption would scare the birds away. None seemed to realize that a wingless photographer would be up there too, with—as one friend remarked—"no visible means of support."

It was spring before I visited the rookery again, a visit purposefully delayed so that the returning herons would gradually become accustomed to the blind without human disturbance. They were there in numbers even greater than their population of the previous year, but their tranquillity was obviously disturbed. Until one landed on the blind, I thought it might be causing the unrest, but then from the original nest the heads of two young Horned Owls could be seen. This association, probably unfriendly, could have ruined weeks of work by driving the herons away from the region. But dispossessing the nocturnal birds by a method other than killing presented a real problem.

Horned Owls as pets are usually unsatisfactory, although I have seen a few, taken from nests soon after hatching, that would fly to their owners and show a slight degree of affection. Some have been trained to falconry and have caught rabbits in free flight for their trainers. But such owls are exceptional for the species. No doubt success was due to a combination of good handling on the part of the trainer and good characteristics of the individual birds. I frankly didn't want to go through the routine of raising baby Horned Owls again and I couldn't find any friends who would admit to having the time or patience to undertake the job. I next called nearby zoos, but their answers were discouraging. Horned Owls, which have a longevity potential in captivity of over twenty-five years, had become a glut on the market, and one institution even offered me any or all of their six-bird surplus.

Then luck hit in an unexpected way when another Horned Owl nest was reported just off a nearby arterial highway. It, like the family in the heron rookery, had two young and the size of all four placed them at about the same age. Here was an opportunity for an unexpected bit of research that might tend to show something about an owl's ability to count and that might also aid future ventures in restocking owls in areas where they have become scarce.

Looking back on that year of herons and Horned Owls, I remember most vividly climbing up and down the tree like a busy elevator without benefit of a protective shaft. Climbing irons and safety belt became as natural a part of my equipment as shoes, and events at the new owl nest did not change this pattern one iota. The second nest was also a tall one, placed in the crotch of a sloping eucalyptus that was jarred disconcertingly by each bite of my irons. As I climbed, the two young above nervously commenced to walk dangerously close to the nest edge, and when I reached its rim and placed the new siblings beside them, both of the original young fluttered to the ground on feeble wings. A half hour later, exhausted from playing elevator, I sat on a rock with three baby Horned Owls beside me, fully realizing that I had been defeated. Their endurance was stronger than mine. Short of sudden death or strong glue there seemed no way to induce all four young to stay in the nest long enough for me to leave the area. Then I remembered Dr. Arthur Allen's work with the Peregrine Falcons of Taughannock Falls, New York, wherein the fledglings were moved many feet to a vantage point for photos. The adults followed them as though such interference were a daily occurrence. Maybe the same scheme would work with owls.

So I climbed the tree once more and for the first time in many ascents the perverse fledgling that had been left in the nest wanted to cooperate, not in the new venture but in the old one, and he tenaciously stuck to the nest as though tied. After finally dislodging him I pitched the entire nest to the ground and reassembled it in a ten-foot-high crotch of a tree about three hundred feet away. For some unknown reason the fledglings liked this new home and all four stayed where they were placed as I walked away. When I glanced back everything was serene. Rubbing climbing iron bruises with hands that were liberally punctured by talons I started down the coast and at the time I had little, if any, desire to ever see those young again.

But you can't work with birds and delve into their lives as I have without developing a compassionate attitude toward them, and as I climbed the hill at Torrey Pines I began to mull over the situation. What if one or all of this quartet had walked off the edge of the man-remodeled home? What would happen to them if they were even then huddled on the ground, their calls unanswered by parents? What if the adults *could* count and upon finding the orphans had pushed them out of the nest, as some-

Western Horned Owl brings a gopher to its young

times happens when small passerine birds discover the unwanted egg of a parasitic Cowbird among their own? A quick turn headed me north again and dusk was imminent as I parked to wait for nocturnal activity.

The young that had been left in crouching positions, looking more dead than alive, were now moving about, and after watching and counting constantly shifting heads I finally came to the conclusion that all four were still on the twig platform. Within minutes darkness descended, blotting out views of the nest. And then, aside from the buzz of insects, all was quiet for the next half hour. Suddenly from the owlets' new home four voices began a frenzied series of rasping hisses, the universal hunger call for most of this nocturnal order of birds. Although I failed to detect the cause of these sharp calls, I presume the sensitive ears of the young had registered the distant call of a parent too faint for me to hear.

Another ten minutes of complete blackness passed, and no matter how much I strained to see the nest where the first frenzied rasping had now changed to methodical repetition, I was really in the dark. Then from an estimated distance of about two hundred feet, I detected a subdued "whoo." If more calls were uttered they were drowned out by frantic answers from the young. These varied in pitch and in my mind's eye I tried to visualize happenings I could not see. Finally, tired of guessing, I switched on the headlights of the car. Far beyond my remodeling job but still within the beam an owl could be seen flying away, and just visible over the rim of the nest the carcass of a cottontail rabbit was being tugged upon by two of the young that shielded their prize from the other two by half opening their wings. Adoption had been successful.

Courtship for most birds usually precedes the nesting season; then, as egg laying begins and incubation commences, ardor cools and energies are switched to protection. Some creatures become overly secretive and silent; others, brazenly defiant of disturbance, actually seem willing to risk their lives to protect their homes. Through some quirk of nature, however, these Horned Owls that had had their family doubled in size through no effort on their part forgot the schedule and for the next few nights displayed a show of amour seldom witnessed.

My first intimation of unprecedented activity occurred the following evening when, after cutting the car engine, I heard the expected silence broken by the hoots, moans, and beak clicking of owls. From the racket I thought there must be six or more of the big birds in on the show and I wondered if the bereaved pair had somehow followed their twins over the intervening miles, but after I became oriented to the surroundings, eyes accustomed to darkness, I located only two adults. One was perched on a massive horizontal branch, and although it hooted continuously I could see by the actions of its head that it was visually following some moving object. With this as a lead I was soon able to discern the male of the pair flitting from branch to branch in a wide circle keeping him about fifty feet from the larger female. Each time he alighted he would face in her direction and bow. His wings would be partially lifted and if the call given was the oft-repeated hoot his stubby tail would rise to a vertical position with every utterance. Occasionally the hoots changed to a maniacal laugh, which was at a higher pitch and almost questioning. When he uttered this strange call only his head would be lowered. Seemingly throughout his gyrations he kept his eyes on the female.

Her notes finally began to vary from the series of disconnected hoots first heard to a whistled "kee-yer" reminiscent of a Red-tailed Hawk's cry but having a throatier quality. These calls excited the male even more, and with a gliding flight he landed about a yard from the female. Her reaction to this close approach I first misinterpreted as belligerent since she spread her wings and held her secondaries and primaries in a vertical position. But when the same pose was assumed by the male I immediately recognized it as a greeting, somewhat similar to that I had seen with Long-eared Owls each time the male brought food to the nest.

The two Horned Owls then slowly approached each other, bowing as they came together and uttering soft "whoos" interspersed with hen-like cluckings that were barely audible from my vantage point about fifty feet away. When within reach of each other, the female, I believe, closed the nictitating membranes of her eyes as she reached forward and nibbled at the male's beak. This part of the romance was similar to one I have seen with several species when a returning mate carries food and offers it to an incubating bird. Now, however, there was no food offering, but instead of drawing back the female lowered her head and the male ran his beak through her feathers in a touching caress, the epitome of gentleness. It was an incongruous sight, especially when one thinks of the descriptive terms commonly used for Horned Owls — "winged tigers," "savage," "merciless," "heartless."

The ritual was repeated for several nights, but gradually the excited tension, so evident when first seen, diminished and finally stopped altogether. Its cessation seemed to coincide with the pair's loss of interest in the site of their first nest. Possibly, therefore, it was a pseudo-courtship brought about by the destruction of the nest but held from consummation and a relaying of eggs by the survival of the young in a different location.

The hunger call of young Horned Owls can be likened to short blasts of escaping steam. The sound is emitted with considerable volume, and several times when searching for Elf Owl nests—whose young can be heard for several hundred feet—I have been led on half-mile trips by baby Horned Owls calling from a distance, but sounding like Elf Owls close by. Even though the various owls differ greatly in plumage, habits, foods, and in many of their adult calls, the hunger cry of all the young is remarkably similar. Possibly this infant voice, lost with age, is a holdover from a common ancestor, just as certain juvenile characteristics in other animals are lost with maturity.

Every second evening for the following two weeks I observed the Rancho Santa Fe owls. To facilitate the work, a small six-volt light powered with a storage battery was installed about fifteen feet from the nest. On the first evening of illumination the adults remained nervous until about two hours after dark, and although they carried food, they would not deliver it until one of the fledglings, hungry and tantalized to the point of being reckless, walked off the edge of the nest in response to their calls.

Their concern with the young one on the ground outweighed their concern with the light and, within seconds after his tumbling fall, both adults alighted on the stick platform and looked down at the owlet. A rabbit being carried at the time was yanked from the talons of one of the parents by the three remaining young, and while the fledglings tore it apart both parents flapped to the ground. After a cursory examination they didn't seem overly alarmed. One flew off into the darkness and the other, with a series of short hopping flights, headed for a pile of brush that had a gently sloping branch protruding from the center.

As I remember the incident now I don't think the adult made any calls on her short journey, but when perched on the sloping trunk she let out a soft rattling call somewhat similar to the protests of a flightless young one that has been lifted off the ground. Those in the nest, engaged in eating the rabbit, ignored the noise, but the owlet on the ground turned toward the sound and ludicrously waddled toward the spot. The gait of a flightless Horned Owl is very peculiar. If you put snowshoes on a bear cub and make him walk on hind legs, the effect might be duplicated; this fledg-

Above, male Horned Owl brings a mouse to a brooding female.
Then, right, the female and her little one
watch the male depart in search of more food

ling was far from being a ballerina. Every twig, branch, and, in fact, imaginary objects brought the bird to a stumbling stop. When he reached the sloping trunk, however, much of this clumsiness vanished as he sidled up next to the owl that had by voice alone guided her young one to the only spot of safety in the area.

A few moments after the fledgling was reunited with the mother, the male delivered a gopher, which was snatched by the young one and swallowed whole. In the next four hours of observation two more pocket gophers and one small rabbit were brought to the young remaining in the nest. All of these food deliveries seemed to be the result of the male's hunting ability. The total tally for seven nights of observation, averaging four hours per night, came to 17 rabbits, 10 gophers, 6 small rodents, 1 skunk, and 1 ground squirrel.

The delivery of this last animal, which is strictly diurnal, surprised me greatly. If it had been brought in at dusk, one might think it had stayed up too late and had been encountered by an owl hunting abnormally early. However, the sun had set many hours before the squirrel was delivered, and I pondered this odd capture until I started to drive home at midnight. Then I remembered: at dusk I had seen a plump squirrel that had been killed by a car about half a mile from the nest. I had briefly considered retrieving it for the owls, but instead I let it lie there. As I drove over the same road at midnight, the animal was gone. Its disappearance and the delivery of a similar one to the young started me guessing. If this creature had been picked up by one of the owls, it formed a hypothetical basis on which to estimate the range controlled by the pair. Guessing that the nest was at the center of the hunting territory, one can figure that these birds controlled at least a square mile.

Although Horned Owls are proficient hunters, probably capable of catching food within a short time after hunger puts them on the move, they are not adverse to taking carrion. There are countless instances of their being caught in steel traps and many of those traps have been baited with an invisible scent. What, if any, part the sense of smell plays in the procurement of foods by predatory birds is not fully understood and needs more research. If it is found to be a decisive factor in getting food, the fondness Horned Owls have for skunks is incongruous. Skunk spray can put the nose of a hound out of business for many hours and sometimes days. Yet Horned Owls are famous as skunk eaters and seemingly are not perturbed or affected in any way by the odor.

At one time I suspected that Horned Owl attacks on skunks were mistakes of identification, but if this is true the birds are slow to learn. There is ample evidence from other observers that some pairs of Horned Owls tackle skunks with such regularity that their feathers or nests are never completely free of the odor. The larger skunks, such as the striped, hog-nosed, and hooded, spray horizontally or at a slightly upward angle, and although evidence is inconclusive they seem to be the species most often caught. The spotted, or Spilogale, smallest of the skunks, would be ideal food for Horned Owls if size was a factor, but I have yet to find any evidence that this species is preyed upon. This might be due to its agile nature, but I am inclined to believe that its trait of running on front feet when agitated, with tail end elevated, creates a unique anti-aircraft device against Horned Owls that blinds them and makes them veer away at the moment of attack.

Many years ago, Dr. Arthur A. Allen noticed that Ruffed Grouse could drum fairly close to Horned Owls and not attract the attention of the predatory birds. For a long time the reason for the owls' lack of reaction remained a mystery. But then one of his students, particularly interested in sonic problems, discovered that a Horned Owl could hear high frequencies acutely but was poor on the low ones. The forty vibrations per second produced by drumming Ruffed Grouse did not register in spite of the fact that many of the calls of Horned Owls are in a low-range category.

For an owl to have a "blind spot" in its hearing seems incongruous, especially when work on Barn Owls has shown that they can catch prey by sound alone. Possibly other members of the family have this same ability or, like Horned Owls, some limitation. What little research has been done on a few species in this family forecasts some amazing finds in the future.

However—like so many of our native birds, and this is especially true of the large ones—the Horned Owl population is dropping alarmingly. Their trait of nesting so early in the season that foliage does not conceal a setting bird contributes to their slaughter. In the past few years three nests in the Tucson region have been found with the adults dead from rifle bullets still sitting on eggs—victims of target shooters. In spite of educational programs by conservation organizations, many of the states protect all owls *except* the Horned. If this attitude toward the birds is not radically changed—and soon—their continued residence in regions that can be reached by jeep, packhorse, or hiking will be soon terminated.

MEASUREMENTS   Length 18–25 inches; wingspread 48–60 inches.

VOICE   To the average person the hoot of Horned Owls and Barred Owls is the best known of all owl calls, so much so that one Hollywood movie—while flashing a Screech Owl picture on the screen—sound-tracked the unmistakable notes of its larger cousin. There were probably few people in the audience surprised to hear the low-pitched "who-whoowhoo-whoooo" supposedly coming from such a bird.

Most of the calls of Horned Owls have a distinctive "whoo" sound. Sometimes it is uttered singly and sometimes in a series that holds the same pitch. Another call occasionally heard in territory where both Barred and Horned Owls reside can best be likened to the bleat of a sheep. In the wild this had me mystified, but recently the breeding pairs at Tucson's Arizona-Sonora Desert Museum uttered this call in the early spring. Another call sometimes heard in the nesting territory is a high-pitched "ank-ank," completely devoid of the rolling "whoo" sound for which these birds are famous. Possibly the sex of all owls could be determined by their calls by a person with perfect pitch perception, but to my untrained ears the notes uttered by both sexes of the smaller varieties sound very much alike. With the Horned Owl, however, there is an easily recognized difference in that the male's voice is pitched three or four half tones lower than the female's—even though females are larger.

NESTING   Horned Owls are not particular about nesting sites and will make do with almost anything available if it happens to be in a territory where they wish to reside. As a result, they have been found sitting on eggs on the tunnel floors of horizontal mine shafts, on the corner rafters of old barns, on the ground under desert bushes affording shade, and even under scrap timber in a busy lumberyard. These places, however, are exceptional and utilized only when there is no chance for a better selection. Their preference in order of choice would probably be: (1) the deserted stick nest of the larger hawks; (2) ledges on vertical cliffs; and (3) in the eastern part of the country, a large natural cavity in a hollow tree. Although Horned Owls usually return to the same area and often to the same nest used previously, they generally vacate an area after three or four years. Their voracious appetite, which depletes available food and forces the birds to move to "greener pastures," is probably the cause. From my observations I doubt if they ever construct their own nests of the twig or stick variety, but instead rely on one built by hawks, ravens, or magpies. In early spring they will often remodel such homes by adding a few green branches to repair the ravages of weather.

Horned Owls are about the earliest nesting birds in North America, often having sets of up to four eggs completed in January. This early nesting brings the young to hunting age in about four months, or at a season when their normal prey—due to the young of the year—are at their maximum abundance. Counteracting this advantage, however, is the lack of privacy for nests in unfoliaged trees. A long time ago this was probably not detrimental, but with the advent of .22 rifles the setting owls now make irresistible targets. Size of egg clutches varies considerably from east to west. Many nests along the Atlantic coast are found with compliments of one or two eggs, in the central states an average of two or three would be normal, and in the far west four or five is not unusual. The average size of over fifty eggs was 56.1 × 47 mm. Horned Owls have one brood a year.

HOURS OF ACTIVITY
In my experience in various sections of the United States and Mexico, Horned Owls have been strictly nocturnal, not venturing forth voluntarily until late dusk. According to Olaus Murie and other arctic explorers, those in the far north carry on their activities twenty-four hours of the day. In temperate regions these birds are perfectly capable of daylight flight, as evidenced by those driven from nests that return during sunlit hours.

FOOD
The prey devoured by Horned Owls varies considerably, depending on the place of residence. They are definitely opportunists, and if they see a chance for easy pickings near a chicken ranch or game farm they can be very destructive. Although I am of the general opinion that man and some of his domesticated animals are the only predators that kill just for the sake of killing, there are cases on record where Horned Owls have obviously exceeded their quota and thus lower themselves into the category of humans. In one case, 106 pullets were killed. There are many other examples on record where Horned Owls have developed a food lust beyond comprehension—especially where they have forced entry into overpopulated pigeon houses, chicken pens, or turkey runs. Killer traits, however, usually appear only when the raiding owl, after entrance, feels himself imprisoned and strikes about blindly.

The predatory prowess of Horned Owls is fantastic and although certain animals listed below are exceptional and not to be considered normal food, Horned Owls have attacked them and emerged victorious. Among feathered prey various ducks, Canada Geese, swans, herons, turkeys, and Guinea Fowl are recorded. Among predatory birds, they have been known to kill Cooper's, Red-shouldered, and Red-tailed Hawks, and among owls Barred, Long-eared, and Barn have become their victims. Charles L. Broley, the Bald Eagle expert, states that they are capable of usurping an occupied eagle's nest. Among mammals, large jackrabbits are common on the menu, and they have also been known to take mink, skunks, woodchucks, opossums, porcupines, and domestic cats.

Below are normal foods listed by Paul Errington in *The Condor* of July 1932, as taken by Horned Owls (in Wisconsin): cottontail, 123; flying squirrel, 5; chipmunk, 1; Norway rat, 28; meadow mouse, 55; deer mouse, 173; weasel, 2; skunk, 2; shrew, 2; Meadowlark, 1; Blue Jay, 1; Flicker, 1; Screech Owl, 1; Domestic Pigeon, 3; domestic chicken, 6; Ruffed Grouse, 2; small bird, 9; snake, 3.

A. K. Fisher's *Hawks and Owls of the United States* lists the foods found in 127 stomachs of Horned Owls as follows: 31 contained poultry or game birds; 8, other birds; 13, mice; 65, other mammals; 1, a scorpion; 1, a fish; 10, insects; and 17, empty. Such a percentage of poultry and game birds probably makes some people believe that Horned Owls in general are detrimental birds that do not deserve protection anywhere; but let's break this list of Fisher's into geographical location by drawing a single longitudinal line through the center of the United States. This would run from western Minnesota down through Corpus Christi, Texas. Of the thirty-one Horned Owl stomachs containing poultry or game birds that he lists, only three were collected west of this central line bisecting the United States. Yet if a person is forced to peruse some of the advertising propaganda of rifle and ammunition companies, Horned Owls should never be protected no matter where they live.

A sensible dissection of facts, which is not based on keeping hunters in the field twelve months a year, would lead to only one conclusion. In parts of the west rabbits have become a problem because of the elimination of most of their predators. Some western states have even paid bounties for jacks and promote rabbit round-ups, which result in the slaughter of thousands of these mammals in a single drive. Yet the same states fail to place Horned Owls on the protected list despite the fact that their prey, with but few exceptions, is made up of crop- and grass-destroying animals, jacks and cottontail rabbits near the top of the list.

A juvenile Horned Owl glides low over a meadow,
scouting for small animals

Snowy Owl

4

SNOWY OWLS

When I was a child, residing at times in Massachusetts, at others on Long Island, I looked forward to each coming winter, hoping that this might be the year of a Snowy Owl invasion. But how elusive these birds were! Others saw them but I always seemed destined to be at the right place at the wrong time. Even the great naturalists Frank Chapman, James Chapin, T. Donald Carter, George Goodwin, and Albert Fisher were familiar with the boy who was "owl crazy," and on each of my visits to the American Museum they were not allowed to forget my passion.

Then came the winter of 1926/27, which in ornithological history was the winter when Snowy Owls appeared in great numbers, making most other invasions meager by comparison. My friends at the museum turned the tables on me. Instead of my pestering them, our phone rang incessantly, and before the winter had really started, eleven of the great white birds were ensconced in my family's basement.

Certain owl individuals I have had as temporary captives have either been wild or tame, and no matter what type of treatment was used, their dispositions rarely changed. This temperament variation of individuals in a single species of nocturnal bird of prey is more or less expected among zoo keepers. But, surprisingly, the eleven Snowys I acquired were not set in their ways. All became gentle within several days and readily took food from my fingers. Within ten days of capture a few would even step from a perch to my bare arm and daintily pick meat from the palm of my hand. When this first occurred I kept a watchful eye on their tremendous talons, which were not only a full inch and a half in length but also needle-pointed and capable of doing real damage with a single tightening of leg tendons. This perching on an arm became commonplace with most of the birds, and I felt those talons only when a shift in my position brought about a clinching action to maintain balance. Even vocal manifestations of displeasure at having human beings in close proximity soon vanished and some were tamed to such an extent that the ominous beak clicking seemed eliminated from their vocabulary.

One Snowy Owl that flew aboard a European liner four hundred miles off the New Jersey coast was exceptionally gentle on arrival in New York. When I went on board to pick up the bird, it was perched on the back of a deck chair with a score of people around it. Some were even fondling his feathers.

This rapid gentling due to enforced association with man is a peculiar reaction for a bird that is usually extremely shy in its arctic nesting grounds. According to Olaus Murie, leader of a United States Biological Survey Expedition to Hooper Bay, Alaska, in 1924, the owls of that area rarely attempted to protect eggs or young by diving at intruders. Yet such heroic actions are not only customary but also to be expected when a night visit is made to the nests of some smaller species of owls such as Screech, Long-eared, and Horned.

The 1926/27 invasion, though marvelous for ornithologists, was a disastrous adventure for the birds. Several I found and watched on Long Island disappeared within a week of discovery, and if there was snow to leave a clue of tracks, human footprints always led from an empty cartridge case to a few white feathers scattered about the owl's favorite roost. This killing reached such proportions that many of my friends stopped bragging about new Snowy Owl locations, fearing that publicity would lead to death. When we consider that the migration stretched from Canada to North Carolina and west to the Dakotas, the number killed is appalling. Aside from a few legitimately taken as scientific museum specimens, the killings were just a form of target practice. And to some hunters, a large white bird, whether it be Whooping Crane, swan, Snowy Owl, or White Pelican, is too tempting to resist.

Spring thaws brought about more butchery, for these owls—admirably protected by a white covering on the earth—could be seen for a mile or so whenever the snow disappeared. I remember one of the birds near Montauk Point at a season when most of Long Island was intermittently covered with light snowfall. As the owl took flight at my approach it passed in front of a dark forested background. If its death had been in mind there couldn't have been a more alluring target, white against black. In seconds, however, it went into a straight glide, low to the ground, and passed over a snow-covered meadow. The bird, so prominent a minute before, disappeared and was not visible again until it crossed a brown spot of ground at least a half mile away.

Despite a protective coloration that worked at times but failed dismally at others, the birds succumbed by the thousands. Many were left where shot, but a "small" percentage arrived at the shops of taxidermists scattered across the northern states. Dr. Alfred O. Gross made a comprehensive study of these killings by checking these shops and came up with the startling figure of 2,363 birds killed and saved as trophies. How many were left where they dropped no one knew. In subsequent years I remember a few taxidermist ads in the sporting magazines. Some showed entire walls lined with these white birds, glassy-eyed in death, birds that are unbelievably beautiful in life.

It is the consensus of naturalists that these southward population movements are caused by temporary periodic scarcities of lemmings and rabbits in the far north, the real home of the Snowys. To visualize this homeland, imagine an area of thousands of miles that is treeless despite an abundance of water; an area seemingly lifeless throughout the greater part of each year but which suddenly bursts into bloom when the rays of an ascending summer sun force a bit of warmth into the frozen soil. Each day as winter progresses toward summer the sun rises higher, stays longer, and finally makes an almost complete circle around the top of the world. Seeds that have survived temperatures sometimes fifty degrees below zero germinate in haste to take full advantage of the short period when it is climatically safe to show blooms above ground.

From hidden burrows small rodents that survived the rigors of winter emerge to take full advantage of a few months of plenty. And the urge to move northward, brought on by lengthening days, affects birds in Hawaii, Mexico, Florida, and all the many points in between. Some creatures, such as the ermine and rabbit, change their white winter coats to more appropriate shades of brown. It is almost as though their basic relationship to southern cousins is still retained even though separated for thousands of years. Others, such as the polar bear, ptarmigan, fox, and, last but not least, the Snowy Owl, are dedicated northerners completely disdaining a change from winter white to a more somber summer garb.

This burst of life is normal around the entire arctic circle, but as in every life zone there are spots where super-concentrations occur. Deltas of the great northern rivers seem to be the focal points even though some remain choked with pack ice for weeks after the birds arrive. And of all these deltas—whether in Asia, Europe, or America—that at Hooper Bay, outlet of the mighty Yukon, is one of the most favored. But a spot accessible to birds can be practically unreachable to a mere human, so the nesting of America's most spectacular owl should be described by Olaus J. Murie, one of two intrepid brothers who have made lasting history in arctic exploration.

The date was March 18, 1924; the place was Fairbanks, Alaska; and the occasion was the meeting of three men—Herbert Brandt, Henry Boardman Conover, and Olaus J. Murie, all making last-minute plans for the most ambitious ornithological expedition yet to penetrate the arctic. The now-familiar bush pilots were unknown at that time. The expedition used dog sleds to cross frozen rivers, permafrost meadows, and glacier-covered ranges. Forty days and 850 miles later the party arrived at Hooper Bay.

In the words of Olaus Murie, who wrote to me when I told him this book was in progress: "This was essentially a flat tundra region, bordering the sea, with numerous hummocks and many small lakes. Here our party found over thirty nests of the Snowy Owl. Most of these were on the high rolling tundra but a certain number were found on the lower tide flats. In nearly all cases the birds chose a hummock for a nesting site, sometimes one that rose up prominently to a height of three or four feet. As a rule a nest was merely a hollow scooped out of the top of the mound exposing the peaty earth underneath the vegetation. Normally the depression was sufficient to hold the eggs but in a few instances mosses, grasses, or lichens plucked from near the nest rim were used for lining. One nest in a small mound capped with tall grasses was really different. Here the adults had torn out enough of the grass to make room for the nest but had left the rest in its upright position. A few owl homes were found on huge granite boulders that adorn the slopes of the Askinuk Range. There construction consisted of scratching off the moss and other vegetation that adorns these mountainside rocks.

"In the Hooper Bay area the height of the egg-laying season seems to be late May.

Snowy Owl prepares a hummock for a nesting site

Snowy Owlets hatch over a ten- to twelve-day period,
thus showing a considerable variation in size and development

Mother Snowy cares for newly hatched owlet

This assumption is based mainly on the finding of four nests on the twenty-fifth of that month. One contained a single egg, two nests had three eggs, and another had five eggs. Only the last of these could be considered a complete clutch, and in subsequent observations we found that Snowy Owls laid every two days, therefore the five-egg nest of May twenty-fifth could have had its first egg laid about the fifteenth of the month. From then on we found many nests and the last we noted with eggs was seen on June twentieth. We were unable to determine the exact incubation period but from scattered observations deduce it to be thirty or thirty-one days.

"We noticed that the Snowy Owl (the female we believe) began incubating when laying started, so in many cases when the last egg of the set hatched the owlet from the first egg was already getting the pin feathers of juvenile plumage. As a result there was a tremendous graduation of sizes of young especially in nests which had eight or ten eggs.

"Most owls lay eggs rather sparingly with complete sets numbering from two to five, but these Snowy nests at Hooper Bay generally contained at least five or six and we found nests with eight, nine, and ten. Now, in theory, the number of eggs in the clutch laid by any species of bird is just enough to maintain a steady or even population. Some birds such as quail will not only lay well over a dozen but will incubate two or more of these sets per year. Such families do not stay large, however, for being ground nesters they are beset with numerous natural hazards. Very few of the off-spring live long enough to reach maturity. So this was one thing we wondered about—why did these white owls have so many eggs when most of the other large owls have so few? As the summer went on we thought we found some clues to explain what seemed to be an obvious overproduction, but this is a phase of Snowy Owl ecology that should have more study before being presented as definite fact.

"Most owls are allies of man, but food statistics of Snowy Owls during the nesting season could very well give a detrimental impression unless we look behind the scenes or, in short, view their diet throughout an entire year. If this were done I am sure that the Snowys would be found to be extremely beneficial to bird life just as the Georgia Marsh Hawks were in Herbert L. Stoddard's monumental works on Bob White. Or as the Roadrunners of Arizona pay their way by their destruction of rodents despite the fact that baby quail are prominently on their menu through a few months in the spring.

"But Hooper Bay, or for that matter, all the arctic is unusual, an area which for a short period has an unbelievable congregation of shore birds, land birds, and waterfowl, including several kinds of eiders, geese, and cranes, all nesting in close proximity. These feathered creatures, due to their abundance, are easy prey for predators, possibly much easier to catch than the two kinds of lemmings and the field mice that are permanent residents of the region. But in spite of this cafeteria where birds are a 'dime a dozen' Snowy Owls still deserve protection.

" 'Look, Olaus, a goose! That owl has taken a goose!' This remark said with wide-eyed horror came to me as my assistant looked into a Snowy Owl's nest. It was an incident which shows the general human attitude toward the so-called predatory species. My companion failed to see all the lemming remains scattered about the same nest but saw only what he wanted to see, the goose. As a matter of fact this was the only goose we found at an owl nest, and geese were abundant in the area.

"Judging from the remains that we found at the owl nests their main food consisted of three kinds of rodents, all of them egg destroyers during the nesting season of arctic birds. We also observed the remains of ducks. Those identified were Oldsquaws. Other birds found at the nests were 2 Willow Ptarmigan, 1 Gull, 1 Cackling Goose, 1 Long-tailed Jaeger, and 2 Short-eared Owls.

"Naturally, in this land of the midnight sun the adult owls were forced to do their hunting in daylight and in this the birds were proficient. However, in actual nest care I believe that it was the more heavily barred female that undertook the duties. The smaller almost pure white males were immaculate but the female with young usually had blood stains below her throat.

"Now let us regress to the egg clutches, which seemed to be abnormally large. As the members of the expedition worked on the natural history of the region owl eggs commenced hatching, but the young became restless within a week or so and often scrambled into the nearby foliage. About July fifteenth the rains commenced and then it was obvious that these wandering young became damp and bedraggled and on several occasions we found their lifeless carcasses after summer storms. Most of the broods which originally numbered seven or eight were in this way reduced to four or five. Some were even further decimated.

"That delicate balance between production and mortality took many thousands of years to reach an equilibrium and it cannot be changed in a hurry. Hence it is conceiv-

Young Snowy in a July rain, a dangerous time
for still-helpless owlets

able that trigger-happy people in the northern states could start Snowy Owls on a slow decline which would accelerate in direct proportion to our explosive increase of humans.

"Possibly, if the birds were seasonal migrants, people would take them for granted as regular winter visitants and guns would not be brought from hiding every time a Snowy Owl was seen. These periodic migrations, spaced about five years apart, however, are welcomed by a new group of hunters every time they occur. Even as far back as 1889/90 one taxidermist 'had five hundred sent to him for preservation.' At that time there were sixty-three million people in the United States and their weapons were primitive. Within a very few years our census will show triple that number and their equipment will consist of adjustable telescopic sights and ammunition with a range that can kill as far as a target can be seen. Frankly, the future of America's most beautiful owl is in jeopardy unless sensible laws for preservation are not only enacted but also enforced."

MEASUREMENTS   Length 20–27 inches; wingspread 54–60 inches.

VOICE   Either the vociferations of Snowy Owls are limited to very few calls compared to most owls, or northern observers have failed to record any but the most important. The many birds I held for a winter before liberation were remarkably quiet. When bickering among themselves they had a high rattling chatter that they also directed at me if I forcibly moved a bird from one perch to another. A short, clear single-pitch whistle was heard occasionally but I was never able to detect its possible meaning.

Reports from various northern explorers tell of a guttural call that might be likened to the notes of ravens. A low "whoo" once or twice repeated is occasionally heard when the birds are in the vicinity of a nest. Thomas Nuttall writes of a "loud, hollow, barking growl, whowh, whowh, whowh, hah, hah, hah (these latter syllables with the usual quivering sound of the owl)." This quivering vibration seems to be a distinct characteristic of all their utterances with the exception of the clear whistle that emanated from my captives. George Sutton mentions calls in the immediate vicinity of nests as "whining in a feeble voice," "an amazing series of laughing barks," "cries which sounded like heavy teeth grinding together."

*A handsome Snowy
lands gracefully on a post*

NESTING   Snowy Owl nests are always on the ground and usually, if soil permits, in a scooped-out hollow placed slightly higher than the surrounding territory. Olaus Murie found a few on the tops of large boulders on slopes of the Askinuk Range, in western Alaska, where the only preparation made by the adults for the laying of eggs was a slight scooping out of mosses and lichens. Nesting material, if any, is usually debris picked up within reach of the setting bird, and as incubation progresses, moulted feathers are added to the nest rim. Thus, when the young hatch there is usually a distinctive circle of white plumage outlining the depression. And, strangely, our only white owl has a short period in its life when it is almost black. This black or sooty down covers them when they are about a month and a half old, making them plainly visible when encircled by a nest lining of white feathers.

Clutches of eggs vary from three or four to as many as thirteen and there seems to be some basis for the belief that Snowy Owls can forecast years of plenty or years of famine. Clutches are usually large when the lemming cycle is about to reach its peak of population and small when these food animals are scarce. As nesting occurs prior to any telltale visible abundance of this prey, the term "sixth sense" is a handy alibi to cover our lack of knowledge on the subject. The eggs, pure white, are somewhat elongated compared to most owl eggs. The measurements of fifty-six eggs averaged 56.4 × 44.8 mm. Only one brood of young is raised in a season.

HOURS OF ACTIVITY   As with all northern owls, daylight flight is a necessity during the months when darkness is never complete. During their spasmodic journeys to the northern United States they seem to retain the trait of daylight activity, having been seen hunting during the brightest periods of the day. Whether such activity is continued after dark is not known.

FOOD   The availability of food, largely a seasonal problem, is what determines the menu for Snowy Owls. During some years in the far north their catches will consist of ground squirrels, hares, and lemmings almost exclusively, with just enough birds thrown in to give them a change of diet. The following year these normal food mammals might be at a low point in their abundance cycle—possibly because of the efficiency of the Snowy Owls and other northern predators. With this temporary scarcity of rodents the ground-nesting birds have a better chance to bring off large broods of young and then, with their overabundance, the food of the owls tends to veer toward feathered prey. Thus from year to year we get conflicting reports on Snowy Owls. Their place in the ecology of the arctic is to balance production and to cut down to livable numbers creatures that are becoming too numerous for their own good.

A. K. Fisher reports that of 38 stomachs examined, 2 contained game birds (Prairie Hen and wild duck); 9 contained other birds; 18, mice; 2, other mammals; and 12 were empty. Although these figures show a slight preponderance of rodents over birds they don't tell the whole story until numbers of each per stomach are listed. Of the 11 stomachs listed as containing birds there was only 1 bird in each. But, in the 20 that contained mammals there was a detailed breakdown of 52 of them. The largest number of prey found in a single stomach was 14 white-footed mice and 3 meadow mice.

Although almost every expert who has spent several seasons in the nesting areas of Snowy Owls avers that small rodents are the favorite food, they also list some catches showing that the owls will tackle any prey they think they can subdue. There are records of them taking full-grown geese, ducks of several varieties, ptarmigan, grouse, and arctic hares. Charles D. Brower, on one of his frequent visits to San Diego, California, reported to me that the Eskimos near his home at Point Barrow claim that arctic fox are occasionally preyed upon and that the young of sledge dogs have been taken.

These large creatures, however, are exceptional items, taken only in dire necessity when normal food is unavailable. In fact, it seems that Snowy Owls do not reside in areas where mice and other rodents are not to be found. This is exemplified by Bering Island. Throughout most of the nineteenth century there were no mice on this insular bit of land and very few owls visited the island. About 1870, however, house and red-backed mice became established and within a dozen years owls became permanent residents.

5

HAWK OWLS

Aside from a very few captives and numerous museum skins, Hawk Owls have completely evaded me. Although they still touch some of the northern states in sporadic winter journeys and I have been tipped off to their presence, the closest I have come to seeing one in the wild was a stump where one had perched the day before. I saw the droppings along with a few sparrow feathers—a recent meal—but, frankly, they were poor substitutes for a living bird—a bird that, according to historians, was comparatively common when the far north was being explored and settled.

A. C. Bent's earliest account of Hawk Owls dates back to 1831, to a quote from William Swainson and John Richardson. Bird namesakes of these two collectors are the Swainson's Hawk and Richardson's Owl (the latter not included in this book because of its similarity to the more common Saw-whet). They wrote of the Hawk Owl: "It is a common species throughout the fur-countries from Hudson's Bay to the Pacific, and is more frequently killed than any other by the hunters."

Half a century later William Brewster wrote of a southern visitation of the birds: "Some idea of the abundance of the birds may be had from the fact (for which I am indebted to Mr. Manly Hardy) that a single taxidermist in Bangor, Maine, received no less than twenty-eight freshly-killed specimens in the course of a few weeks." In the

American Hawk Owl

same year Ned Norton said: "Hawk Owls came three weeks ago in greater numbers than ever seen before. Farmers' sons have been killing them all over the country."

The easy kills may have been due to the fearlessness of the Hawk Owl, as described by Spencer F. Baird, Thomas M. Brewer, and Robert Ridgway in 1905. Relating the experience of a Mr. Dresser, who observed the species in New Brunswick, they wrote: "It showed but little fear, and could easily be approached within gun-shot. When shot at and missed, it would take a short flight and return to its former perch. On one occasion, Mr. Dresser, firing at one with a rifle, cut the branch close under the bird, which returned almost immediately to another branch, was a second time missed, and finally fell under a third shot."

Call it misplaced trust or stupidity, for both terms have been used in describing the Hawk Owl's utter lack of fear, which was probably developed through ages of association with northern Indians who hunted and killed only what they needed to survive on. Hawk Owls were not eaten so the birds led a carefree life. But the new breed of humans that invaded their territory was different; and early-day scientists, who conceived of a comprehensive collection as hundreds of similar skins laid out in cabinet drawers, roamed from muskeg to muskeg eliminating each resident pair.

If the collecting was done during the nesting season, the so-called stupidity or trust inherent in these owls was then combined with reckless valor, which made the birds make dive after dive to protect eggs or young. If these had been nocturnal instead of diurnal owls a strike at the head under cover of darkness might well have had the desired effect in making humans vacate the territory. Long-eared, Screech, Horned, and some other owls have put me on the run on several occasions, for there is a big difference in human bravery if an attack comes from ambush on a pitch-black night or from a creature that can be seen and ducked in time.

This characteristic valor shown by Hawk Owls when protecting a nest is well exemplified in a 1919 account by Archibald Henderson of Alberta: "As I climbed the stub she charged and knocked my heavy Stetson hat off and struck me several times on the top of the head and quite hard. Once she put her claws through my shirt and scratched the skin. I had to watch her continually and wave her off when she charged, always straight at my head, as I was cutting out the side of the stub to get a picture of the nest and eggs. The mate appeared on the scene soon after I commenced work, but did not attack like the other."

Hawk Owl fearlessly attacks photographer

Dr. Joseph Grinnell found two nests in northern Alaska in 1900. I quote his words on the valor of the owner of the second nest found: "When I tapped the tree the bird left the nest, flew off about thirty yards, turned and made for my head like a shot. It planted itself with its full weight onto my skull, drawing blood from three claw-marks in my scalp. My hat was torn and thrown twelve feet. All this the owl did with scarcely a stop in its headlong swoop. When as far the other side the courageous bird made another dash and then another before I had collected enough wits to get in a shot. The female, which was evidently the bird I had first discovered on lookout duty, then made her appearance, but was less vociferous." From the two accounts above it is plainly evident that the birds are foolishly fearless, and unless a rapid evolution in behavior, favoring more "cowardly" individuals, takes place, they cannot long survive.

After the early collectors had taken their toll, sportsmen followed, and as their routes were along the waterways and lakes the adjoining muskegs were worked over some more. In the early 1900's a scarcity of the birds began to be noticed over most of Canada, and A. G. Henderson's report (1919) of breeding quite commonly near Belvedere, Alberta, showed that it, of all the provinces, still maintained a sizable population of the birds. But even this population did not exist very long, for in the early 1930's Bent received this message from Frank L. Farley in Camrose, Alberta: "The Hawk Owl has become exceedingly rare during the past twenty-five years." Farley in the past had seen as many as thirty in a single day, perched on the tops of trees and haystacks watching for mice.

Abundance, rapid decline, and now virtual disappearance seems to be the history of this trusting bird. Despite the fact that present-day bird photographers have penetrated every cranny in North America, good photographs taken in the wild of American Hawk Owls are as rare as the bird has become over most of its former haunts. Therefore, because of a paucity of recent information, most of this chapter has necessarily been based on observations made by the old-time naturalists, who usually considered a bird in the hand worth many in the bush.

As a breeding bird, Hawk Owls — even in their days of abundance — probably rarely nested south of our Canadian border states. From there they existed northward to the limit of trees and the start of the tundra. Although some reports mention the finding of eggs in stick or twig nests constructed by other birds, most explorers say that the

Nestful of Scandinavian Hawk Owls

Hawk Owls preferred the hollowed end of a broken branch. They mainly inhabited the muskegs of the northern forests, which were surrounded by poplars, spruce, pine, birch, willow, and alder, where in a falcon-like pose the birds perched upright on a dead stub on the watch for mice.

The falcon characteristics do not stop with perching attitudes. Because of the Hawk Owls' semi-pointed wings and direct flight with quick wing beats they have been compared with Peregrines by one falconer familiar with both birds. In speed of flight, though never officially timed to my knowledge, they are fast—possibly faster than most if not all other owls. Another falcon-like trait is their ability to hover motionless in a manner similar to the hovering of a Sparrow Hawk. The large falcons, such as the Peregrine, Prairie, and Gyr, have a tendency to drop from their eyries to gain flight speed before horizontal flight. Hawk Owls also use this system for take-off from a branch perch or a hollow-log nesting cavity, and from twenty feet a Hawk Owl will drop almost to ground level before beginning horizontal flight. From the attack accounts of Henderson and Grinnell, it even seems that this owl's method of protecting a nest is similar to that used by the Peregrine guarding a nesting eyrie. From the words of these naturalists the only difference I can detect is that the Hawk Owl's swoops of anger are on a horizontal plane, while those of the large falcons are vertical dives. It also seems that the Hawk Owls hit an intruder more often than they miss. Peregrines rarely make actual contact.

MEASUREMENTS   Length 14½–17½ inches; wingspread 33 inches.

VOICE   Attempting to translate the calls of birds into words has always baffled me. Aside from the calls of Killdeer, Whip-poor-wills, and a few others, I have always had to hear the calls before I could decipher what the combinations of letters printed in popular bird books were supposed to represent. However, never having heard or even having seen a Hawk Owl in the wild I will list the calls as others, more fortunate than I, have heard them.

Archibald Henderson says: "The calls of this Owl are a trilling whistle, *wita-wita-wita*, etc., which is the love call of the male. I have never heard it uttered by the female. It is one of the signs of early spring, being first heard in February and through March and April. Other calls are *squee-rick* or *quee-ick*, *wike* or *rike*, and *wherr-u*." Lee

Raymond Dice writes: "Notes and calls are numerous and quite varied, but all seem quite musical. *Kr-r-r-r-e-e-eep*, a low rapid rattle rising to a cry, is often heard. *Wur-a-wur-a* (rapid) and *kuk-a-wuk* (very low) were given by a male on March 25th while he was seated in a dead spruce." C. B. Horsbrugh says: "My specimen gives voice to a melodious *wheup, oop, oop, oop, oop, oop*, generally at dusk." Ernest Seton says that "it sometimes utters a rolling *whil-ill-ill-ill-loo*, somewhat like the cries of the Long-eared Owl."

NESTING   By far the great majority of Hawk Owls' nests found to date have been in rotted cavities at the ends of broken branches or at the tops of treetrunks. That the birds occasionally use stick nests, which have probably been deserted by Goshawks or Horned Owls, is doubtless true. But such sites, at least in the last half century, are the exception and not the rule. Strangely, however, Oliver Davie in his book *Nests and Eggs of North American Birds* intimates that the great majority of eggs collected in the early days were taken from stick nests in the tops of trees. It is illogical to suppose that nesting habits have changed in a century of time, but possibly there were areas where stick nests were preferred and other areas, explored at a later date, where hollow-ended stumps were often utilized. An analogous situation could have occurred with Ospreys. Early explorers along the Atlantic coast would have termed them tree nesters, and in dead trees at that. In the Gulf of California, however, which is only now being adequately explored by ornithologists, most Ospreys nest on cliffs or rocky promontories.

The eggs of the Hawk Owl, which are dull white in color, are rounded oval in shape, with the long diameter averaging 1.53 inches and the breadth 1.25 inches. Four, possibly five, would be the average number in a clutch but occasionally larger sets, up to nine, have been found.

FLIGHT   The name "Day Owl" has almost become synonymous with "Hawk Owl" because of its diurnal habits. There are records of Hawk Owls following farm equipment in bright sunlight to reap a harvest of the mice scared out of hiding by the machines. Many museum specimens of the species, collected at midday or later, have held freshly killed food when their stomachs have been examined. A. C. Bent writes under the caption "Behavior": "It probably hunts more extensively by day than any of our other owls, except, possibly, the short-eared and the pygmy owls." Its flight, which has already been discussed, is falcon-like, being direct and fast. The bird is also capable of hovering after the manner of a Sparrow Hawk.

FOOD   Although almost all evidence points to small prey, such as mice or sparrow-sized birds, as the normal food for Hawk Owls, these predators are capable of changing to larger quarry when necessary. A. K. Fisher writes: ". . . when the snow is deep and its favorite food is hidden, it follows the large flocks of ptarmigans and subsists on them." Edward Forbush says: ". . . it has been seen to kill and carry off a Ruffed Grouse." Archibald Henderson writes: ". . . when driving to Edmonton, I noticed one which had just caught a large white weasel or ermine. I wanted the weasel and tried to scare it into dropping it by shooting, but there was nothing doing and it flew away with its prize."

OF SPECIAL INTEREST   Hawk Owls have so many characteristics setting them apart from most other owls that they almost seem to be a family of their own. They have not only a speedy flight on pointed wings but also evidently endurance enough to carry them great distances. This is to be expected in a normally migratory species but not in a bird that is known to be sedentary. American Hawk Owls, however, have on several occasions been taken in England and there is even a doubtful record many years ago from Bermuda.

Although most owls have long been known to use their highly specialized eyes in the capture of prey, it is now being discovered, largely through the researches of Payne, that ears too can play an important part in the procurement of food. For this phase of hunting many owls have ear openings extremely large for the size of the head. They are usually hidden from sight by the facial disks. The Hawk Owl, however, is evidently not endowed with such auditory prowess, for its ear openings are small, no different from those found in most other species of birds the same general size.

Although the numbers of Hawk Owls have been reduced considerably—almost to the point where they should be included in the growing list of endangered wildlife—legislation of the past few years may give them an added lease on life. Most of the states in the United States have laws protecting all birds of prey, and this trend is being followed by some of the provinces of Canada. The streamlined Hawk Owl needs as much protection as possible, since it has the characteristics of both hawk *and* owl.

6

PYGMY OWLS

INTRODUCTION After several years of diligent but unsuccessful searches for Pygmy Owls throughout the valleys in the Sierras, I heeded the advice of some naturalist friends and stopped at Yosemite. The park naturalist, "Bert" Harwell, was conducting a tour and as the entranced group adjourned at the bear-feeding pit I begged him to spare just a few minutes to show me a Pygmy habitat. Without moving from the spot, he commenced to call, and as his repetitive "whew" whistled into the darkening trees I thought of the many miles I had covered in real wilderness for just a glimpse of the bird. People were still clustered about in noisy groups and although I tried to be optimistic, grave doubts clouded my thoughts. I couldn't by the widest stretch of the imagination picture a "rare" owl in such surroundings. And then there was an answering call from a branch above.

Two minutes later the bird, whose kind had evaded me, was at eye level, talking back and repeating every note that Bert uttered. Now, a quarter of a century later, when I think of Pygmy Owls Bert Harwell becomes an integral part of the mental picture. Furthermore, in searching the literature I find that most of what is known about this diminutive species of owl comes from observations made in the Harwell domain, and largely with typical all-out Harwell help. As a result, the man, before his death a

few years ago, became a veritable storehouse of knowledge gleaned through the years. Without his invaluable aid, personal observations in this chapter would be woefully lacking. Despite the twenty-five years that have passed since seeing my first Pygmy Owl, the birds, as wild creatures, have remained almost legendary to me, known almost exclusively by call but not by sight.

BERT HARWELL ON PYGMY OWLS
To actually pinpoint a spot where any secretive bird has its densest population takes plenty of guesswork, for many factors enter into any bird census. The chief one to be considered is the availability of the country to competent observers. There are many valleys in the California Sierras that are inhabited by Pygmy Owls, but from research published to date the beautiful valley of the Yosemite seems to have the most plentiful supply. Whether this is fact or fancy will probably never be known but I am inclined to believe that the Yosemite observations of Mr. and Mrs. Charles W. Michael, F. C. Holman, Leo Wilson, Dr. Harold C. Bryant, William Leon Dawson, Dr. Joseph Grinnell, Dr. Tracy I. Storer, and a host of others well known to the birding fraternities are what have made the Valley Pygmy Owl headquarters.

These observers have shown that there are many characteristics of Pygmy Owls that tend to separate them from the rest of the family. First comes their habit of diurnal hunting. This is a trait to be expected from owls that range far to the north where the midnight sun creates long days. But just why these diminutive inhabitants of warmer life zones should subject themselves to the abuse of other diurnal birds is an unanswered question. There seems to be no doubt, however, that most Pygmy Owls spend a large part of their nocturnal hours sleeping within the confines of woodpecker holes. Another trait of the birds, strange for such small predators, is their choice of food. In size the Pygmy Owls are midway between two notorious insect eaters—Elf and Screech Owls—but during the nesting season these "in-between creatures" switch from prey-to-be-expected to birds.

Possibly the combination of small birds on the summer diet and diurnal habits has some connection with a peculiar feather pattern that makes Pygmy Owls two-faced. All owls abroad during daylight hours either by choice or necessity become targets for diurnal birds, and there are numerous cases on record where owls have been killed by the repeated pecks of their tormenters. In almost every recorded observation, how-

Pygmy Owl pokes its head from its nest —
a woodpecker hole

ever, the attacks have been launched from the rear or from the blind side, just as owls usually attack humans disturbing nests from any direction except face on.

Charles Michael, formerly the postmaster at Yosemite, said after watching an adult Pygmy: "With a lightning movement he would turn his head halfway around and we got the impression that the owl was double faced; for when he turned away his face we saw a second face on the back of his head—a white beak and closed eyes under beetling brows. Close scrutiny showed this beak to be a white feather and the eye brows and eyes produced by an arrangement of feathers . . . This make-believe face was a very good one, and we wondered if nature had bestowed this second face upon the little owl to fool his enemies." Michael's wonder sounds logical, especially when we consider the mimic "eyes" on the tail end of caterpillars, on the wings of butterflies, and on the sides of some fish.

The choice of a life in daylight also seems to have changed Pygmy Owl eyes. Most of the owls that are awakened in bright sunlight have their pupils "stopped down" to mere pinpoints, which, brown-eyed owls excepted, are surrounded by wide circles of yellow iris. But with Pygmy Owls, even in full glaring light the pupil contraction is slight. When, to this dark-eyed appearance, the jaunty but insignificant tilted tail of a house wren is added, Pygmy Owls are arrestingly different from other owls.

In the Yosemite region and possibly in other areas almost all nests of the Pygmy have been discovered in tree cavities previously excavated by woodpeckers. The entrance size preferred is that which is made by the acorn-storing variety of woodpecker. Despite this owl's use of such homes, many observers remark on the amicable relationship of the two birds. Smaller woodpeckers, however, not only cuss out the owls whenever found but also have been recorded as food for the owls.

The Pygmies' dependency on the holes of woodpeckers, birds that will nest at almost any height, makes their home-site elevations vary from low to high. Some have been found at least seventy feet up, and others within six feet of the ground. Although some of the nests observed at Yosemite were used for only a single season there are a few records where holes have had yearly occupancy. Even though these owls are forced to accept what they find in the way of cavities their choice of ideal habitat seems to be a meadow or open area surrounded by trees. Such an area has a variety of life of all kinds that allows the owls, especially when feeding young, to vary their menu.

The range controlled by a pair during the nesting season is probably fairly small.

Rear view of a Pygmy shows "eyes"
on the back of its head

Pygmy in flight

This is deduced by conversations with a number of observers who have remarked on the scarcity of normal food prey in the immediate vicinity of a Pygmy Owl nest. This to a certain extent emphasizes the skill of the birds as hunters and also shows that they do not forage far afield to obtain prey for their young. From a human viewpoint one of their methods of obtaining food is not strictly according to Hoyle, for on several occasions they have been seen to drag fledgling Downy Woodpeckers and Sapsuckers from their nesting cavities. Unfortunately it takes only one or two observations of nest robbing to create such descriptions as fiend, villain, rapacious, bloodthirsty, but actually this little owl usually follows accepted rules of hunting.

In flight these owls resemble shrikes not only in the beating of the wings but also in size, and, like the shrikes, their pursuit of prey is usually direct. When not hunting, the owls' flights are generally short and consist of rapid sallies from one lookout point to another. Unlike most owls, their wingbeat swishes are audible, because they are not overly endowed with a soft wing lining, but as evidence on Elf Owls and Burrowing Owls indicates, silent flight is seemingly not essential to insect eaters. Possibly the trait would also be a wasted evolutionary effort for birds that habitually hunt by daylight.

Pygmy Owls catch feathered prey on a seasonal basis—usually when young owls are in the nest. Throughout the rest of the year these owls prey mainly on what we might term expected foods—grasshoppers and other insects in the late summer, small rodents when insects are unavailable. But even on this logical menu the size of some of the prey they tackle is fantastic. There are records of them killing rodents of such size that they could not lift them off the ground! A few of these David and Goliath battles have been witnessed by observers, and the system seems to be for the owl to grab and hang on tenaciously. In one case a rodent of pack rat size was dropped onto one end of a twenty-five-foot log. The owl gripped the hind parts of the struggling prey and as the mammal ran the owl spread its wings and tail to create a drag. Two minutes later and at the far end of the log the rodent tired sufficiently for the owl to dispatch him with a twisting peck at the base of the skull.

Some of the Yosemite observers have even seen Pygmy Owls attempt to make contact with the local Douglas squirrels, but whether these dives were bona fide or just bluff is not known. There is at least one authentic case of a Pygmy tackling a weasel, but in this encounter the challenger was killed in the battle. Evidently their valor in obtaining food is based on optimism and if they think they can conquer they will try.

Definitely reported foods are: mammals—chipmunks, mice, and pack rats; reptiles—small snakes (at least up to one foot in length), and numerous lizards; insects—a tremendous variety, with grasshoppers leading the list; birds—vireos, Sapsuckers, Downy Woodpeckers, Purple Finches, various warblers, Marsh Wrens, towhees, blackbirds, juncos, and Pine Siskins. I know of one case in which a captive Pygmy killed its cage mate, which was a male Sparrow Hawk. Since nothing would surprise me about them, I am glad Pygmies are one of the smaller species. Give them Horned Owl size and proportionately increase their nerve and confidence, and even people would be afraid to tarry in Pygmy Owl habitats.

Many of the Yosemite observers have remarked on the Pygmy Owl's trait of storing the remaining portion of any prey too large to consume at one meal. Some of this so-called storing might be due to the extreme size of the prey caught, which is lifted by main force and supported in a tree crotch when hunger is the real incentive. When hunger is somewhat appeased, however, the frightened owl is liable to fly off and leave his partially eaten food behind. That the bird ever returns to such a cache has not to my knowledge been substantiated.

MEASUREMENTS   Length 7–7½ inches; wingspread 15 inches.

VOICE   Until Bert Harwell's friends in Yosemite made observations on Pygmy Owls there was a dearth of information on their calls. Surprisingly, most of the researchers call the varied utterances songs, a term that would be ridiculous if used on most of the other members of the owl family. To quote Mr. and Mrs. Michael: "The song of the Pygmy Owl is a series of mellow notes, rolled along at an even pitch. The first stream of notes comes rapidly in a sort of low rolling trill. Then comes a pause and three notes each separated by a distinct pause. In print the song might be represented as follows: O-O-O-O-O-O-O-O-O-O—OO—OO—OO. The characteristic feature, the touch that gives charm and beauty to the theme, is those long hesitating pauses between the last three notes. There is also a ventriloquistic quality to the voice of the Pygmy, and the least turn of his head apparently changes his location." Another call of the Pygmy, which has a questioning intonation, consists of a single whistled "whew" that ends abruptly with just a trace of raspiness. A soft twittering note is sometimes uttered when a bird is disturbed. A long trill, somewhat rasping, is also reported.

*Most Pygmy Owls, like this one,
live in former woodpecker nests*

NESTING   As mentioned by Harwell earlier, Pygmy Owls nest almost without exception in the deserted homes of woodpeckers. Some observers mention twigs, pine needles, and other materials in the bottoms of the nesting cavities. These in all probability are refuse left by former tenants and not purposefully brought in by the owls. There are a few records of nests being used for three or four years, but most experts feel that the voracious appetites of Pygmies over a small range soon decimate their prey animals and the birds are then forced to find new locations. Egg clutches number from four to seven. They are white and quite similar to those of Mourning Doves, although slightly larger and rounder. The average size of two dozen eggs was 29.6 × 24.3 mm. As far as is known, Pygmy Owls raise only one brood per season.

HOURS OF ACTIVITY   Although the calls of Pygmy Owls are often heard at night, the owls are mainly active during twilight hours, just before dusk and soon after dawn.

A captive I borrowed from K. C. Lint of the San Diego Zoo for behavioral owl study was kept in a cage measuring about twenty by thirty feet. It was completely covered with intertwining grapevines, which gave the owl many secluded perches. During daylight hours he was easily located by tossing a mouse in the air, which he would hit as soon as it touched the ground. But at night reactions changed, for despite food offerings, he refused to emerge from one of his many hiding spots. Each night for a week, after many painstaking searches, I thought the bird was gone—which now makes me question their supposed rarity. Later I learned to mimic his call, and his immediate answer, even after dark, was reassuring and a clue to his whereabouts.

FOOD   As Bert Harwell has mentioned, the food of the Pygmy Owl changes drastically from month to month and preference is not necessarily tied to a depletion of prey relished at a previous time. All available records indicate that small birds are a nestling food and are the chief nourishment of the young until they attain flying age. After they are on the wing, however, grasshoppers and other insects claim their attention even though feathered prey is still abundant. In late fall rodents are pursued and form the bulk of their diet until the breeding season and a growing family swings attention back to small birds.

7

ELF OWLS

The sighting of an Elf Owl, Mearns' Quail, or trogon is a must for the army of amateur ornithologists that visit southern Arizona each year. Momentary glimpses of the quail are usually the reward if a day or so is spent walking the mountains at five or six thousand feet. Even the Trogons with their limited state population of less than twenty or thirty pairs will cooperate if certain of their well-known canyon habitats are visited. But the Elfs, smallest owls in the United States, can be almost mythical, remaining as invisible as that proverbial needle in a haystack. And this seeming scarcity exists despite the fact that their range not only corresponds to the range of the giant saguaro cactus, which stretches in a wide belt along the international border from eastern Arizona to California, but also beyond in many areas. Where these plants grow, the population of Elf Owls is probably heavier than that of any owl on a range of similar size.

It might seem incongruous that the smallest and most delicate of owls should voluntarily live in a region as uncompromisingly harsh as the desert, a region that evolved the world's largest wren and the strangest of cuckoos—the Roadrunner. But to understand the "why" of this tiny owl's selection of homeland, investigations of the "how" must be made, delving into the ecology that makes its residence possible. Such curiosity leads directly to the saguaro cactus, and from there to other birds, and thence to rainfall, to heat, and to cold, *ad infinitum.*

Compared to most of the United States the saguaro belt is a relatively dry area, with an annual rainfall of about twelve inches falling in two distinct seasons, mid-summer and late winter. The latter, ending about March, occurs at a time when the migratory Elf Owls are in warmer southern climates, where their type of food is not affected by cold. These early rains are slow and steady, with single storms covering thousands of square miles. Wasteful run-off is at a minimum and moisture absorbed by the ground during this season is of extreme importance to plant growth later in the year.

Then comes a four-month period of drying out. Grasses carpet the desert and annuals burst from the ground at the first hint of warmth. Fuzzy rounded tops of saguaros become bumpy with buds while each branch of the ocotillos is topped with a red candle-flame flower. This can be a period of plenty. If the winter overcasts "did right" by the desert, all its mammals store fat, energy for later use, and the region is the rainbow's end for returning migratory birds.

The days of late April or early May are alive with song as males compete for favors and after winning compete with others for nesting sites. The clear-cut wolf whistles of the thrashers change to melodies, interrupted by the sad coos of Mourning Doves or the more sprightly notes of the larger White-winged Doves. Even the ground squirrels get into the act as their trilled whistles from ground level rival the songs of trained canaries.

Early in this period of activity there is a special night when the Elf Owls arrive. Evidently their journey northward is not a series of solo migrations but instead must be one of massed flight that brings them all into the region together. Then for a week or so their low whistles, puppy-like barks, and notes that might be construed as songs issue from all regions where there are saguaros and up into mountain canyons where there are cottonwoods and sycamores. Woodpeckers at this time are subjected to a strange insomnia—a sleeplessness induced by owls poking their heads in hole after hole investigating possibilities for suitable nests.

These holes don't just happen, as do some of those found in sycamores, oaks, or other deciduous trees, but instead are the result of a fortuitous set of circumstances that necessitate a delicate cooperation between woodpeckers and cactus, timed to fit into a short period following the winter rains. During precipitation the long horizontal roots of saguaros gather in moisture and store it in the massive trunks. The vertical indentations or grooves so prominent in the dry season swell and almost flatten because of the moisture pressure within, which occasionally becomes so great that the plants have been known to split.

However, after this moisture has been stored for several weeks it tends to thicken, finally attaining a consistency that scabs over and protects any injury to the cactus. This change occurs when the urge to excavate homes becomes an obsession with Flickers and Gila Woodpeckers, and on a plant such as the saguaro—which can be chopped to bits with a blunt hammer—home building for these birds is messy but not necessarily difficult. The sharp-beaked birds bore straight in six or seven inches, and then down to about fourteen, where a bulbous chamber is formed. All during their work and for days afterward, the ton or so of plant that towers above drips moisture into this new cavity. Some settles on the bottom, but most of it solidifies on contact with air, forming a hard internal shell that, strangely enough, is more durable than any other part of the living plant.

So it is that the industry of two birds, unknowingly picking a season when their work will be most tolerated, permits Arizona to boast a monopoly of the smallest of owls. These hard-shelled nests, suspended in a fibrous fluid of watermelon consistency, are used for a season or so by the architects, but in time the original artisans move elsewhere. Then the deserted homes are utilized by any one of a dozen other species, including Elf Owls, the undeniable favorites of people who know them.

Although these nests repel the juices of the supporting plants and therefore make the desert the habitat for many birds, they can also be death traps. The attribute of being water-tight means that they hold water, and every few years gusty unseasonable rains create pools in the bottom of these chambers, several inches deep, which ruin clutches of eggs and drown nests of young. But despite the occasional failures, there are other benefits to the saguaro nests, only recently discovered at Tucson's Arizona-Sonora Desert Museum.

On a trail within the grounds of this institution, devoted to desert lore, an aged saguaro has a thermometer inserted into the center of the trunk. Another is suspended outside. The latter has varied its readings by as much as fifty degrees in a single twenty-four-hour period, dropping sharply at night and climbing to better than 115° at noon. Inside, things are more uniform. Sudden rises are prevented by the plant's

evaporation of moisture and on unbearably hot days the readings remain at least twenty degrees below the outside high. On cold nights, the warmth of the day lingers on—held evenly at a similar twenty degrees or so above outside temperatures by the slow cooling of the tons of water stored within. When it is realized that prolonged highs of 106°, or lows of about 90°, can injure eggs that should be maintained at close to 100°, saguaro values, despite faults, give these plants a definite ecological importance in the desert's scheme of nature. If the phrase "key to life" were used on the desert, as it is for the coconut palms on Pacific atolls, saguaros would fit the parallel precisely. Without these majestic plants many desert animals would be forced to move elsewhere or perhaps would not exist at all.

Within a few weeks after the mass of Elf Owls arrive from the south they pair off, select home sites, become almost mute, and drop their inquisitive ways—once again permitting woodpeckers to get a full night's sleep. If audible clues at this time are criteria, it would seem that the Elf Owls have moved elsewhere, for aside from the rarely uttered low whistles they keep their whereabouts a secret until the three or four white eggs in each nest have hatched. This event tends to stimulate vocal utterances, but it might be that such an effect is due to the hunting activities of both adults instead of just one, which is the case during the three or more weeks of incubation.

Deception, probably unintentional, is exercised when Elf Owls fly from low bushes to seek a higher vantage point on a towering cactus. The perching place for such a lookout is usually at the entrance of an unoccupied cavity, a fact I failed to grasp until I had lugged heavy ladders over many miles of desert. Preference for such perches is probably due to the diligent work of the original excavators in breaking off the sharp points of all spines surrounding their homes. But perhaps the owls are unconsciously utilizing a protective coloration, for their brown feathers blend with saguaro scars to perfection.

At an age of about three weeks some of the infant down covering young Elf Owls is forced loose by a growth of feathers. From then until flying age small bits of this white fluff occasionally reveal nest locations by becoming impaled on the mutilated spines at nest entrances. Detection by this method, however, is purely happenstance, a bit of luck that cannot be relied on. At this writing, after finding well over fifty nests in fifteen years, I have learned an easy way. The first requisite is not thinking of the birds until July first, for this decision will eliminate a lot of needless ladder carrying. A perus-

*Two birds that, by digging out holes, make it possible for Elf Owls
to nest in saguaro cactus—the Gilded Flicker (left) and the Gila Woodpecker*

al of the next few paragraphs is heartily recommended for those with a life list that does not include Elf Owls.

Normal growth of the young continues until their size cramps the quarters within the cavity, making any motion or exercise almost impossible. At a similar development of those species that use branch nests the young would be seen exercising wings at every opportunity. This confinement of the Elf Owls, however, creates restlessness that is appeased only by climbing the inside walls. By the end of June, one or more of the fledglings begin nightly vigils perched in the doorway, even though their first flights from the saguaro home are one or more weeks away.

Before this partial emergence, Elf Owls, like the young of most other species in the family, utter rasping hunger calls, but three or four inches of soft saguaro flesh insulate and absorb the sounds so that they barely reach the nest opening. However, when the young are at the doorway, the rhythmic rasping hiss radiates over the desert for three or four hundred feet and on still, windless nights may be heard at twice the distance. It's a peculiar call, at times almost ventriloquistic, and at others so light that a listener wonders whether wishful thinking is playing tricks.

It was while following one of these rasping calls in the rugged canyons of Arizona's Kofa Mountains that I first became acquainted with Elf Owls, and with beginner's luck watched an adult obtain food in a novel but very efficient way. Each time I believed that the general direction of the hunger call had been located I would move to another spot and relocate the note. With four or five of these changes in position it was then possible by simple triangulation to pinpoint the nest to a single cactus.

On one of these position changes I was leaning against the towering flower stalk of a yucca, the only object in the area spineless enough to permit such familiarity, when I was suddenly showered with insects. At the same instant vibrations were telegraphed down the thick stalk to my hand. A quick but guarded glance upward disclosed an Elf Owl in an upside-down position, pecking at the underside of the flowers, from which bugs were still dripping in profusion. The moment my flash beam hit him he was off and away, voicing with low barks and whistles his displeasure at being disturbed.

After brushing beetles, wasps, and moths from my shoulders I proceeded to the point determined by triangulation and found the nest. And again—beginner's luck—it was low, only fifteen feet from the ground with the entrance facing an immediate steep rise of the terrain. A stand to support me at nest-hole height, along with cameras and reflectors, was easily constructed and the rest was up to the owls. If they would cooperate, photos were assured.

As with the Screech Owls, however, I questioned the advisability of suddenly surprising the birds with a large box. If the tales of their extreme shyness were true, I might frighten them away for good. That night, however, I found that my fears were groundless. Nothing short of cutting down the saguaro would have caused these birds to leave, and within minutes of climbing on the platform one of the adults used my shoulder as a perch. Throughout the remainder of this short four-night study, something either mechanical or human was a regular resting place for both birds on their feeding.

These birds, whizzing by my ears on delivery trips, eight to a dozen times an hour, shattered one of my old pet theories. Prior to this work, I had believed that all nocturnal members of the owl family were capable of almost noiseless flight, but the swish of Elf Owl wings may be heard when the birds are still twenty or thirty feet away. In subsequent work with Burrowing Owls and limited observations of Pygmy Owls I have found that these two species also are not silent in flight. All three feed to a great extent on insects, seemingly in preference to most other foods. Could it be that the much publicized flight is a wasted attribute when such quarry is the prey, and that these three gourmet specialists are losing the ability?

The Kofa pair of owls also disclosed another skill, that of hovering on rapidly beating wings with body motionless in a helicopter-like flight. This ability is also executed by Burrowing and Pygmy Owls. Perhaps other owls similarly hover on occasion, but I have never seen them do it. Hovering, however, is a flight technique highly developed among the insect-eating birds, and that there is a tie-up of this flight with foods seems to be more than coincidence.

During the first three nights of observation I was kept busy changing films, replacing bulbs, and meticulously trying to list all the foods brought in by the adults on their average of about ten trips per hour. As the observations continued, the latter became monotonous—moths, beetles, scorpions, and occasional centipedes.

Despite the monotony of diet, however, the volume was wondrous; it didn't seem possible that the few acres controlled could supply so much food, food that to the human eye was almost nonexistent.

By mounting a camera on the complex construction above,
the author secured the picture at right. It shows an Elf Owl with a scorpion

And then I thought of that cluster of beautiful agave blossoms that rained insects upon me just before the nest was located. Was it the cafeteria that aided them—like the light for the Screech Owls, the city dump for the Flushing Barn Owls, or the occasional highway-killed animal for the Horned Owls? I decided to cut one of the flower stalks and prop it near the blind, where its ten-foot height would then be at my eye level.

During the moving, insects of many kinds showered from the petals, but many followed along and sought their familiar hiding places as soon as the stalk was fastened to the platform. Dusk brought more, and when nightfall induced the owls to activity each of the thousands of blooms trembled from the motions of the myriads of creatures seeking nectar or pollen. Many were wasps, hornets, or small bees, insects not especially conducive to peace of mind when one's space is limited. But these worries of the early evening were minor compared to those created by a hungry Elf Owl that hovered for a moment and then zoomed under the cluster. There, hanging upside down, the wings beat a violent tattoo on the blooms above. Insects of many kinds clouded the air, and for two or three hours after this attack I moved about gingerly while both birds reaped a harvest from the ground below and from the platform.

Almost half of the insects dislodged from the tier of blossoms were wasps or hornets, but on this last evening of observation, I failed to see the owls pick up or show interest in any stinging type. In view of the number of scorpions delivered, this seemed strange. That the birds should feed their young creatures that have caused death to humans but completely disdain an insect that would only cause temporary pain, was illogical. Baffled by this incongruity I left the Kofas and was not enlightened until more than a decade later.

Then, on a trail at the Arizona-Sonora Desert Museum, the nest photographed by Disney for his masterful film "The Living Desert" became reoccupied. For at least two years Gila Woodpeckers had been the interim tenants, but when they moved on, owls returned. This was a handy nest, perfect for the museum to give visiting bird watchers a glimpse of these secretive owls, and when used in conjunction with the famed wildlife blind it helped immeasurably in spreading the institution's fame.

I believe it was Dr. Roger Carpenter, at that time an ecology student at the University of Arizona, who first mentioned the peculiar condition of the tails of scorpions brought by the parent owls to this nest. All during the previous night, he, along with

Elf Owl on an agave blossom

other students, had checked foods, using powerful binoculars and telescopes to pull the birds into range. The prey, in numbers of individuals, was tremendous. In variety, however, it differed little from the Kofa list, the only important addition being a few of the seven-inch desert centipedes. But the scorpions, grasped by the owl's bill at the upper end of the body, failed to hang right. The whipping tail in life and death usually has a curl upward so that the bulbous poison sac and its stinger points toward the center of the arachnid's back. The tail, however, hung straight down. Closer scrutiny disclosed some of the appendages mangled beyond recognition, while others had the danger end cut off as though with a razor. Thus, deactivated, these lethal creatures were made safe for the young, and fifty percent of my ten-year-old question was answered. But the other part, the "how" of the capture, and the method of mutilation, still remains an unsolved mystery. It is still being worked on, however. If I hear the call of an Elf Owl I now look for a scorpion, and—hope. Or if I see a scorpion I listen for an owl—and hope some more.

MEASUREMENTS   Length 5–6 inches; wingspread 15 inches.

VOICE   The Elf Owl is not a species that freely advertises its presence by calls, and were it not for a few individuals that habitually break the rules these owls could well be termed exasperatingly mute. There is only one short period—a week or two in late April or early May—when, arriving in numbers from the south, they bicker among themselves for nesting sites. That this is a busy period in their lives is indisputable, for there have been times when I have stopped just to listen and was able to detect the calls of ten or more birds in the darkness around me. These calls didn't come from compact ranks but instead were spread over the desert, some so far away as to be barely audible. I am relatively sure this vocalizing was prompted by nest hunting, for I also occasionally heard the churring notes of a disturbed Gila Woodpecker, and night calls from these birds are rare at any other time of year.

A couple of months of silence then ensue, when the female is incubating eggs or caring for tiny young and the male is hunting and delivering food. During this period the birds converse in such low whistles that the sounds cannot be detected unless an observer is extremely close. Aside from a few rare pairs that are nonconformists, an owl silence reigns on the desert and is not broken again until the first days of July approach. Then the young, which have been in the bottom of the nest, attain strength enough to climb to the opening and so get free of the sound-muffling walls of the living cactus. On a still night their rhythmic hiss of hunger penetrates the darkness for several hundred feet. From the calls of the young, and only these calls, a fairly accurate census can be made. On one night about fifteen years ago I found eleven nests by letting the calls of the young be my guide, whereas several weeks before I had found only two, by diligently using a clueless search technique.

NESTING   When I first started to work with these birds, the world's smallest owls, I—like many observers—believed them to be a species compatible only with saguaro cactus. As saguaros were where I first found them, it was to saguaros that I returned to do further work and I even published work stating that the plant and bird were never very far removed. Later investigations, however, by Joe T. Marshall, Jr., Allan Phillips, J. David Ligon, and others, have proven me wrong, and I am now wondering if typical desert plants on desert terrain are really population centers, or if they are in reality just an overflow from the wooded hills of the Catalinas, Rincons, Santa Ritas, Chiricahuas, and other mountain ranges in the Elf Owls' over-all domain. My record of detecting eleven saguaro-situated nests in one night has been exceeded several times when similar searches have been conducted in cottonwood, sycamore, and oak stands on the slopes of desert mountains.

The great majority of nesting hollows used are the deserted holes of woodpeckers, ranging in size from Gilas to Flickers. The excavation made by Ladder-backs, which is often placed in an agave bloom stalk, seems a little too small to accommodate the owls. Occasionally, however, Elf Owls will occupy a hole that has been enlarged by a Screech Owl or Sparrow Hawk. Some of the photos illustrating this chapter were made at the Kofa Mountains at a saguaro nest with an opening about four inches across.

HOURS OF ACTIVITY   Elf Owls seem to be one of the truly nocturnal members of the family, rarely if ever flying in daylight unless disturbed. Their daytime retreat, however, does not have to be a secluded cavity; it is often a branch near the trunk of a dense tree or bush, frequently within several feet of the ground. During their northward migration, great numbers of them, sometimes three or four to

Elf Owl delivers a centipede to its nest

a bush, have been seen near the city of Hermosillo, Mexico, where during daylight they sit tight and can almost be picked off the branches by hand.

Parent owls near a nest that is being disturbed after nightfall will often flit about with undulating, almost woodpecker-like wing beats. Their normal flight, however, is very direct and usually performed close to the ground. I believe that most of their hunting is done from lookout perches, even though they are capable of hovering motionless in the air like Sparrow Hawks. When thus suspended on beating wings there is an audible whirr of feathers despite the fact that the leading edges of their primaries have some of the deadening fuzz that makes most other owls almost silent fliers.

FOOD   These birds, being tiny, naturally have the smallest of prey on their menu. From my own observations I would guess that about fifty percent of their food consists of insects. Grasshoppers, crickets, and beetles are common, closely followed by caterpillars and small moths. The other fifty percent, in bulk at least, is made up of various scorpions, including the occasionally deadly centruoide and the nondeadly centipede. Mervin W. Larson of the Arizona-Sonora Desert Museum staff observed and photographed them bringing six-inch centipedes to the nest hole. These were carried dangling from the beak and just before the nest entrance was reached a braking action of the owl's wings slowed the speed of the bird enough to permit the flexible body of the centipede to slip forward. At just the precise moment the bird's speed would increase again and the owl would follow the straightened-out food into the nest.

As mentioned earlier, many of the insects are caught by using agave blooms as cafeterias. I have never seen Elf Owls deliver wasps or stinging bees, which are also drawn to these flowers, and I have yet to witness their system of deactivating the stingers of scorpions or of subduing centipedes.

Albert Fisher lists a small mammal and twenty beetles as found in the stomach of one Arizona Elf Owl. In the Kofa Mountains I saw one carry a canyon tree toad into the nest, and on another occasion at the same nest what looked like the carcass of a worm snake, although it may have been a centipede.

OF SPECIAL INTEREST   Since writing the preceding pages, an excellent work by J. David Ligon has appeared on Elf Owls, published by the Museum of Zoology, University of Michigan, No. 136. Ligon's work from his base at the American Museum Southwestern Research Station in the Chiricahua Mountains has shown, as previously pointed out, that a sizable population of Elf Owls exists not only among desert saguaro cacti but also in the oak-pine-sycamore association of some desert mountain ranges.

In addition to exploding the misconceived theory about Elf Owls being dependent only on saguaro cacti, Ligon has proved false the idea that Elf Owls rely on hollows for daytime roosts as well as for nesting. He found that those owls in wooded areas roost during daylight hours in densely foliaged trees or bushes. He also determined that the female begins roosting in the cavity (selected by the male) one or two weeks before the laying of the first egg, but that the male continues to pass daylight hours in dense brushy growth. The fact that saguaro-based Elf Owls have markedly different roosting habits is probably the result of extreme temperature fluctuation and the lack of dense foliage, for many desert plants either shed their leaves entirely during the hot season, or have leaves so small that the birds would not have any protective cover. The availability of cavities may also have a bearing on the daylight roost of the males, for the woodpecker-used saguaros often have so many holes that the plant is virtually a bird apartment house. The temperature leveling effect of saguaros on the lower deserts could be the irresistible attraction in an area where daylight temperatures often exceed 110°.

Ligon further discovered that the first spring arrivals from their then unknown winter home were males, which were soon joined by the females. And, after several years of comprehensive study, he has come to the conclusion that the earliest arrivals tend to populate the low saguaro areas first, and later arrivals the foothill regions and progressively on up to an oak association. Ligon states in his thesis that "the more southern populations and those of lower altitudes breed somewhat earlier than do birds that nest in mountain canyons." Some, but not all, Elf Owls should be incubating by April fifteenth. In the saguaro areas around Tucson the young are ready to leave the nest between the last week in June and the end of the first week in July, and three and a half months later, about the middle of October, adults and young disappear from the area, not to return until March or later.

To locate the winter home and thus either prove or disprove a migratory nature, Ligon made a winter examination of a number of cavities that Elf Owls had inhabited

A row of baby Elf Owls

the previous years. All were empty, so he started south. At every likely-looking spot, tape recordings of Elf Owl calls were played, but he got no responses from wild birds until he reached the southernmost portion of their known breeding range. In this way he finally determined that their winter home extends east from northern Oaxaca, west to southwestern Michoacan, north to the edge of the Mexican plateau near Cuernavaca, Morelos, and south to the Sierra Madre del Sur in central Guerrero. He also states that on their winter range the owls apparently roost in bushes or shrubby trees during the day. In most areas where Elf Owls were found in his winter investigations there were no large trees or cacti to provide cavities suitable for roosting. Their earliest return to Arizona, according to Allan R. Phillips, has occurred on February 16 and 25.

POPULATION DENSITY   The compilation of accurate figures on the population of any living creature is at best subject to guesswork, and this is especially true for those that are nocturnal. However, if any one set of creatures is observed in the same territory over a period of years, trends of abundance, or scarcity, may be detected, even without hard figures.

Some years ago, when I first started working with Elf Owls, I soon came to the conclusion that in their saguaro territory they probably had a population density greater than any other owl in the world. As mentioned earlier, I found eleven nests one night in approximately one square mile of desert. The area was bordered by the Tucson Mountains to the northeast and overlooked Avra Valley to the southwest. The Arizona-Sonora Desert Museum had just come into being and aside from its few buildings, lights of human habitation were practically nonexistent. Six or seven miles away the flat Avra Valley floor had a few tilled areas where farms were experimenting with cotton, milo maize, and safflower. Aside from these distant scars, the country was essentially the same as it had been when pioneers started to settle the region.

The summers of 1954, 1955, and 1956 brought to light more nests, and in retrospect I feel sure that the eleven-nest record could have been topped in any of these years. However, the number of farms increased rapidly in the valleys, and now it takes three or four nights of diligent searching to find the homes of four or five of the diminutive birds. Fifteen years ago each nest found had from two to four young. Now the average has dropped to one or two. That there is a correlation between the owls' progressive decline and the ever-widening use of insecticides in the valley below seems sure, since similar patterns of bird depletion are being reported from many other parts of the world. Note the nesting Peregrine Falcons, completely gone from the Atlantic coast; Brown Pelicans that failed to raise young off the coast of California; and as this is being written, Ospreys along the Connecticut shore have virtually been eliminated. Is the Elf Owl to join the list of the endangered before adequate laws put a stop to this poisoning of the world?

Burrowing Owl

8

BURROWING OWLS

Burrowing Owls, by some standards of comparison, may not be the most unusual members of the family, but by their choice of cellarette homes, their daylight activities, and their quaint and beguiling ways, they stand at the top of the list as true individualists. Across wide and varied areas, from deserts below sea level to isolated colonies in Florida, and to the rolling mile-high plains near Denver, they are known by a dozen different names. The "How-de-do Owl" of the cattle country is the "Billy Owl" of the farmlands or the "Gopher Owl" of Florida, showing that people all across the owls' wide but broken range consider them extra-special birds.

But despite the fact that they are about the only members of their large clan that perch in open view without becoming lifeless targets, their numbers have decreased alarmingly. Some conservationists have even included the species on the critical survival list. In a strange way, however, this decrease is not so much the result of thoughtless target practice as it is due to the owls' being a lethal by-product of the killing of other animals.

Take a quick backward look at our "limitless west," a term widely used until a few years ago, and compare it with today. Millions of buffalo were munching and migrating from one area of plenty to another. They didn't have to be driven from pasture to pasture to prevent overgrazing beyond redemption, for their stomachs told them when to move before irrevocable damage had been done. Now they are gone. Over this vast, once unfenced, land there is now barbed wire, and confined within are millions of cattle trampling over the same trails until furrows are worn deep, nibbling the same grasses day after day and never giving the earth a chance to rest and recover. Every drop of nutrient is wrung from the soil to feed the appetites of a human population explosion that can end only in disaster. If prairie dogs nibble grasses and thus threaten the cattleman's dollar, shoot them. If grasshoppers cut greens and become competitors with cattle, poison them. Don't look to the future, but try to get more than your share today. In fact, don't look to the past—to the dust bowls that followed two world wars, created by an idiotic belief that one sixteenth of the earth's land mass could feed one third of the world without dire consequences.

Now flying over the former well-balanced haunts of the Burrowing Owls there are airplanes spraying millions of dollars' worth of lethal mixtures. For decades it has been done with a foolish abandon, only matched in stupidity by the meager research sums allotted to study the over-all effects of insecticides before they were loosed upon the world. On the ground veritable armies of poisoners seek out the last of the prairie dogs, and now this animal, which once numbered millions, is almost a mythical creature. Their tunnels, which permitted water to seep into underground reservoirs for the feeding of wells hundreds of miles away, are clogged and useless.

Once an imbalance is created, its effects snowball. Every Meadowlark, Horned Lark, nighthawk, plover, magpie, quail, Sage Hen, or Burrowing Owl that habitually eats poisoned grasshoppers succumbs also. This causes a vacuum of birds, which draws others from unpoisoned areas, and they in turn meet the same fate. Today's dispersal of insecticides and poisons has gone far beyond the concern of only the rancher; it is everybody's business, and is the main reason for the extremely beneficial Burrowing Owl being placed on the list of vanishing birds.

But here and there some still survive, mainly on the ranches or farms of the small segment of our human population that believes in a "live and let live" world. Chance led me to such an oasis as I wandered aimlessly along roads of eastern Colorado. Daylight was only a few hours old and the white cap of Pikes Peak, eighty miles west, drew my attention; but as I watched, the slithering form of a prairie rattlesnake in a rut ahead made me put pressure on the brakes and bring the car to a stop. For a moment

An adult Burrowing Owl perches on a prairie dog mound

the reptile coiled and then gracefully proceeded on his way, heading for a small mound that I had failed to notice until the direction of his travel had pointed it out. Beyond was another, and another; and as my gaze wandered over the flat prairie a whole colony of mounds materialized in the distance covering about a quarter square mile in area. Watchful waiting was soon rewarded by activity as prairie dogs came to the surface, peering from their burrows to see if the coast was clear. When twenty or thirty of them were in sight, a lone owl hopped to a mound on the outskirts of the colony.

Here in a relatively confined area and during a short space of time a rattler, an owl, and prairie dogs had appeared, all directly concerned with the burrows of this last; I was seeing a mixed society on this Colorado prairie. If the early pioneers had viewed this set-up for what it was—merely a convenience for snakes and owls—instead of concocting a story of one big happy family, a yarn that's still prevalent and exaggerated with each retelling would not be so firmly implanted in people's minds.

Most nature myths are comparatively easy to dispel with unbiased research and observations. But this owl–snake–prairie-dog yarn has great tenacity, and unfortunately, bits of circumstantial evidence seem to give it factual support. As a case in point, I remember returning to the prairie dog village that the road-crossing snake had helped me locate. Activity visible when I approached ceased when I set the handbrake and only a lone "How-de-do Owl" remained on the surface of the ground. Within a few moments, however, the rodent population commenced to emerge from their burrows. In ten minutes the animals were foraging for grasses many yards from their individual homes.

Then came sudden panic as the creatures scampered for cover; each twitch of a prairie dog tail brought a bark, or each bark brought a twitch of a tail. I have never been able to decide which comes before which, for it almost seems that the vocal cord is knotted to the rear appendage. A lone owl and several prairie dogs fought for the chance to scramble into the same burrow together as a hawk swooped low over the now seemingly abandoned village. Heads reappeared almost instantly and then prairie dogs in all parts of the colony scampered away from emergency havens sought in the face of danger, and ran for their own individual burrows. But in the moment of village-wide fright I had seen one part of the myth apparently verified—prairie dogs and owl within the same hole.

And in natural history literature there is abundant verification of rattlesnakes using holes occupied by owls and prairie dogs. The late C. B. Perkins, collecting for the San Diego Zoo, caught about three hundred prairie rattlesnakes in three days' time, within a quarter-mile radius in the heart of an occupied prairie dog town. He pinioned some of these to the ground between burrows, but most of them—sometimes four or five at a time—were hooked from actual burrow entrances as the snakes emerged from hibernation. According to this herpetologist there had been prairie dogs on many of the mounds before he disturbed them by his presence, and soon after he completed each day's chore rodents and owls came to the surface again.

But despite the cases offering irrefutable evidence that prairie dogs, owls, and snakes use the same burrows, there is none that supports the myth that these three characters live as a happy family. In an emergency, perhaps, the old saying "any old port in a storm" holds true. But otherwise each species tries to control its chosen home. This is not only my conviction but also the reasoning of many other naturalists when arguing the point with laymen who are adamantly opposed to our thinking. It is a tough myth to crack, because observations have to be made in the wild and underground, where the harmony is supposed to exist.

For the next few days nesting owls of the region had to cope with a new and invulnerable enemy as I proceeded from burrow to burrow and probed a long wire into darkened tunnels. I had plans for a new type of photographic observation but an owl-occupied burrow was needed with a reasonably straight entrance, one in which I could accurately measure the depth and distance to the nesting chamber beneath.

Most of the tunnels turned sideways. Some rose, a few dropped and doubled back in contortions that completely baffled my probing wire. Then luck followed despair. Two feet below the ground level and four feet in, the wire trembled violently. By turning it slowly I could feel it scrape the hard shells of eggs beneath an incubating owl, an owl that was vainly trying to fight the wire away. For an hour or so I calculated the depth of the nest, based on the length and angle of my metal probe. Then, to be sure, I calculated it all again, for I had learned that tunnels ideal for my purpose were the exception and not the rule.

About a foot behind the spot where the chamber was presumed to be I carefully dug straight down. After removing two cubic feet of earth I tunneled horizontally toward the nesting chamber with the utmost care, for the success of my study would

Burrowing Owl inside a prairie dog burrow

hinge largely on the success of this excavation. When I hit the nesting chamber at floor level I was probably more elated than the Hudson tunnel engineers when their two test runs touched beneath the river. After placing a tin protectively above the eggs to prevent damage from cave-in I removed the entire roof of the nest, replacing it with a pane of glass. This permitted the entrance of sunlight for about an hour at high noon. All during this work the "How-de-do Owls" went through their ludicrous performances, bowing repeatedly from nearby mounds. If my glance was not obviously pointed in their direction they would stand sedately without much show of motion, but they were quick to realize when they were the object of my fixed gaze. They would then rise to their fullest height, bow suddenly two or three times, touching their breasts to the ground, and nervously fly to other mounds, giving voice to their chattering cries.

Some of these far-flung perches were the mud caps of occupied prairie dog burrows and when the worried birds landed on these I received my first indication that prairie dogs could be intolerant. A few actually ran to their burrows and shouldered the trespassing birds into flight.

After a wait of several days I returned to the nest, wondering whether the owls had continued housekeeping in the face of my intrusion. Both were near the nest opening, but although I waited and watched from a distance they failed to go underground. Before leaving I lifted the glass and felt the eggs in the chamber below. They were warm, showing that one of the birds had recently been incubating. The next day at dawn the camera was placed in position and then the waiting really started. It was a test of endurance. At times while lying under the canvas and staring into the ground glass I was about to concede that the owls would win.

The first view of the old bird in the chamber was a great surprise. I had been flat on the ground for hours and thought that I knew just where on the surrounding terrain each adult was perched. As I glanced into the Graflex, however, I was suddenly astounded to see an adult straddling the eggs and glaring into the camera lens. I reached down very slowly and pushed the release. The noise was too much for the bird's nerves; it jumped straight into the air and tried to fly through the glass above. When the reflex mirror was pulled down again the parent had disappeared; I thought at the time that the bird had left the tunnel. In a few minutes, however, a head appeared and yellow eyes glanced about the nesting chamber. I took one more picture, which again frightened the bird into the darkness, so I called it a day, afraid to press my luck too far.

A week or so later I was back again. Both birds had become accustomed to the man-made changes, and aside from viewing the uncovered glass above with alarm they went about their home life in an apparently normal fashion. If one of the pair was incubating, its mate would come to the entrance of the burrow and call whenever it captured some dainty morsel that it wished to share. The one below would then get off the eggs and go to the surface through the tunnel, but on several occasions it viewed the glass above as though meditating a shortcut. The faintest movement of my hand toward the camera release brought about a beak snapping and a ruffling of feathers in an attempt to drive me away. It was after the young had hatched, however, that the heroic actions started.

When I looked through the camera, and saw several downy white chicks next to the remaining eggs, a parent bird was crouching above them, weaving from side to side and doing everything to make a small body look ferocious. At the click of the camera the adult charged, and leaning against the partition that separated the camera from the nest chamber, it beat upon the glass with rounded wings. For the next hour or so the bird was so quick to attack at the slightest movement of my hand that I took no photographs. Then the sun cast a shadow on the nest and I was forced to stop observations.

With the passing of several weeks the young grew considerably and were spending much of their time running about the chamber and tunnel. One lone egg of the clutch was infertile and the fledglings used it as a practice target to improve their footwork. From almost any spot in the chamber they could stab out with their absurdly long legs and grasp the white object. Sometimes they would reach down with their beaks as though they were plucking off imaginary grasshopper legs, but as a rule they were satisfied to use the egg solely for practice.

About this time in the young's development, I noticed that some of the insect food was brought home still full of life. Beetles had their abdomens crushed and the grasshoppers their jumping legs removed, but both were still able to cover the ground at a slow crawl. It seems possible that this practice serves the purpose of helping the young learn to catch their own food.

In a period of an hour and forty minutes the young were supplied with the fol-

Underground, a Burrowing Owl crouches protectively over eggs

lowing items: 22 grasshoppers, 17 beetles, 2 lizards, 1 frog, and 1 jumping mouse. Another catch for about an hour included a small garter snake (these are water-loving reptiles and the nearest water was over three quarters of a mile away), and one striped spermophile, as well as the usual number of grasshoppers and beetles.

Then I got a surprise. While the adults were foraging for food I noticed that the glass separating the camera from the nest needed cleaning. As I reached toward it there came from the chamber a noise so closely resembling angry rattlesnakes that I instinctively jerked my hand back. The chamber was empty, however, with no sign of a reptile of any type. The heads of some owlets within the tunnel were barely discernible, and it was from that direction that the sound issued.

The "rattle" came from a bird whose throat was vibrating rapidly. Each time the throat stopped pulsating the clear-cut noise of a rattler would stop. Naturally the yarn of the "happy family" came to mind. Couldn't this sound very largely explain it? Rancher friends normally not given to exaggeration had told me time after time of hearing rattlesnakes immediately after scaring young owls into a burrow. This had been related so often that I was glad to find it was actually based on fact, even though the "fact" had been misinterpreted in the telling.

About a week after the young became proficient fliers the ranch was deluged by one of those sudden rain storms that convert dry gullies into raging rivers. The nest and tunnel became a hopeless muddy mess. But even in this minor disaster I learned more about Burrowing Owls. The following morning fledglings and parents had gathered together on a prairie dog mound about a hundred yards away. Fom afar I realized that they were waging a battle for possession of the burrow. Each time the rodent owner of the burrow came within about twenty feet of the mound an adult owl hovered on rapidly beating wings. And at the slightest intimation that the prairie dog was going to make a shouldering rush to the entrance the bird would swoop and rake its back. After several attacks from above the prairie dog seemed to lose interest in repossession and when I approached for a closer view it sought refuge in a burrow many yards away.

So my experiment produced no evidence to give validity to the belief that there is a "happy family" relationship among these three animals. Throughout the weeks of intermittent observation two thirds of the cast (prairie dogs and owls) were in constant sight, but their actions, when crowded, definitely showed that harmonious feelings did

Two baby Burrowing Owls in their underground nest

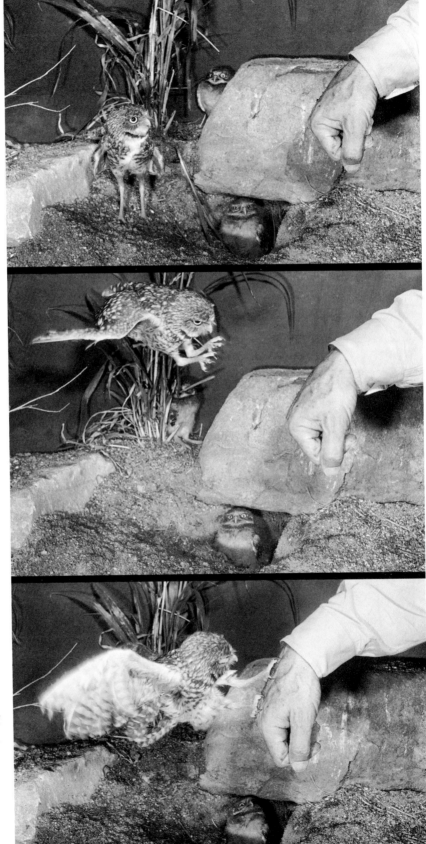

Burrowing Owl
on the attack

not exist. The rattlesnake, third member of the group, failed to put in an appearance but a perfect imitation of its familiar sound had been created by the fledgling owls. I can't help but feel that this instinctive sound mimicry formed the original basis for the yarn, and that even to the present day—when heard but not investigated—the astonishing mimicry perpetuates the false story.

Perhaps the birds do nest in holes that have been used by reptiles, and perhaps rattlesnakes hibernate in holes that were formerly the nests of owls, but in either case the tenancy is successional and not simultaneous. There are only a few days in the spring and a few in the fall when snakes are concentrated about prairie dog colonies. Throughout the remainder of fall, winter, and early spring, the reptiles are deep underground in slumber until warmth permits them to disperse across the countryside.

MEASUREMENTS   Length 9–11 inches; wingspread 24 inches.

VOICE   Although Burrowing Owls are primarily diurnal, they evidently do not waste much time sleeping at night if their calls may be used as a gauge. Before and during the nesting season the nighttime call most often heard has the plaintive tonal quality of a Whip-poor-will. By letters it might be represented as "oo-coo" with the last syllable drawn out. Two alarm calls are used. The first, which the owl uses when only mildly disturbed, has an almost chicken-like "twut-twut." When danger becomes imminent, a rapid "cack-cack" is uttered, usually while in flight and so fast that it seems continuous rather than a series of broken syllables. On the few occasions the parents made half-hearted dives at me, or when they dived at coyote, badger, or prairie dog, a short lisping "zip-zip" is uttered at the moment of closest approach. When cornered in a burrow they have a rattling scream, the adult version of the rattlesnake rattle emitted by the young.

NESTING   From all the records that I have been able to find, Burrowing Owls nest underground. Most of these nests consist of tunnels previously excavated by mammals with a nesting chamber as far as ten feet in, slightly enlarged by the owls. This is used as a repository for the eggs. There have been a few records of their use of storm drain pipes along roadsides as nesting sites but as a rule such man-made holes are used as sanctuaries in case of danger. Until the Burrowing Owls at the Arizona-

Sonora Desert Museum established the first captive breeding records for America I was of the opinion that they were not capable of excavating their own nesting chambers, but when the urge occurred our pairs were proficient and fast.

There is some tendency to colonize, both during the nesting season, when a half dozen pairs may occupy as many acres, and in winter, when as many as a dozen birds may be forced to retreat into a single burrow. As with most ground-nesting birds, Burrowing Owls lay large clutches of eggs — from six to eleven, so this use of a single wintering burrow may be occupancy by a single family group. Although the eggs are white, averaging 31 × 25.5 mm, they are usually so stained as to be a blotched tan until washed. Much of this discoloration comes from the uneaten food refuse brought to the incubating parent. Many of these underground nests also have a wide variety of miscellaneous matter. Elliott Coues reports scraps of dead animals such as pieces of an antelope skin, parts of a coyote, and a two-foot-long snake skeleton. The burrow entrances are always covered with the legs of grasshoppers along with powdered cow and horse dung, which is also used on the floor of the nesting chambers.

HOURS OF ACTIVITY

Burrowing Owls can be active twenty-four hours a day, but most of my research on the prairies of Colorado tends to show that they are mainly diurnal. Some proof that activity ceases during hours of darkness may be deduced from foods found at the Colorado nest. Grasshoppers, for instance, usually remain hidden at night and without movement are difficult to locate. But during seasons of grasshopper abundance they constitute well over half of a Burrowing Owl's diet. The small uta lizards, which turn in at dusk and emerge at dawn, were another favorite prey and they probably formed about fifty percent of the reptilian diet of the owls. Such evidence of increased daytime activities is of course circumstantial, but the open areas frequented by the owls under my observation made night study difficult and, due to human presence, inconclusive.

Other naturalists, working on the same species in other localities, have voiced varied opinions regarding their hours of activity. Charles Bendire, for instance, says: "They hunt their prey mostly in the early evening and throughout the night, more rarely during the daytime. As soon as the sun goes down they become exceedingly active, and especially so during the breeding season." Frankly, when I consider the food statistics that follow, gathered by other investigators, it seems that no rule can be made about a Burrowing Owl's hours of activity. Availability of prey, type of prey, and individual differences of the birds themselves present too many variables.

FOOD   Albert Fisher's report says that "of 32 stomachs examined, 3 contained small mammals; 3, lizards; 3, scorpions; 1, a centipede; 30, insects; and 1 was empty." The food statistics taken by other naturalists have approximately the same ratio, so there is no need for repetition. However, a report from William Lloyd of western Texas is interesting in that he found some Burrowing Owl nests containing the remains of Bell's Vireo, Savannah Sparrows, and other birds, so possibly availability is the key to the diet of individual owls that will feed on any creature they are capable of subduing.

Spotted Owl

9

SPOTTED OWLS

INTRODUCTION A few years before Arthur Allen's death, he and his son David spent several weeks with me on the desert around Tucson. Their parabolic reflectors and tape recorders were busy not only from dawn to dark but also well into the night when the calls of owls were to be heard. During our work we often mentioned Barred Owls and their western relatives, the Spotted Owls, for I had done only meager work on this prominent genus. Weeks later, after a lecture tour farther west, Dr. Allen stopped by again and regaled me with accounts of a pair of wild Spotted Owls that had been tamed to the point where they would take food from fingers but otherwise carried on their normal life seemingly oblivious to the presence of a human being.

I begged for the name and address of his contact, but he stuck to his promise to reveal nothing of the identity of his friend. She remained anonymous and the location of the nest an unrevealed secret. One concession was made, however. He would write and get her reaction to making an exception of me. Several months later she arrived at the Arizona-Sonora Desert Museum. We talked of birding in general, in Arizona, California, and Mexico, and although I did not realize it at the time, I was being tested to see if I could be trusted with information concerning one of North America's least-known owls. Evidently I passed with flying colors. Gradually we warmed to a conversation about Spotted Owls and the taming of them while they remained free in a forested wilderness. The revelations disclosed by her study of Spotted Owls were so astounding that a chapter by her became a "must" for this book.

But immediately I encountered trouble, for the pair of owls still resided in her study area. We reasoned that spreading knowledge about the owls would encourage conservation. However, opposing this idea was the ever-present fear that if the location of the study were made public, the lives of the owls might be jeopardized, for Spotted Owls are much-sought-after birds. To get just a glimpse of one, bird watchers would make cross-country trips time after time and if successful, would consider their efforts well worthwhile. Any such disturbance could drive the birds from the area. Unfortunately, rarity begets value and, like certain Lincoln pennies, the lifeless skins or the blown eggs of Spotted Owls are much in demand.

We were in a quandary. I wished to give credit for work so well done, but the author's only thought was for the well-being of the owls. Her approval was finally given with the proviso that the chapter be credited to "Anonymous" and nest location mentioned only as "somewhere in the range of Spotted Owls"—a range extending from British Columbia to old Mexico and from the Pacific coast east to New Mexico.

However, several years have passed since the conversation which settled upon an anonymous author. The pair of birds that were the subject of almost a decade of study have either lived out their normal life span or have moved to another area. With their former domain deserted, through no lack of a human friend, credit may now be given where credit is due. The author is writer-photographer Grace Maddock Miller, who recounts here her experiences with North America's least-known owl.

Note: Barred and Spotted Owls are closely related, the former being the eastern counterpart of the western Spotted Owls. For this reason, only the life history of the western species is included in this work.

GRACE M. MILLER ON SPOTTED OWLS   For seven years I was an adopted member of a family of western Spotted Owls in a more or less avuncular capacity. The members of this family, one that changed in number of offspring each year, were attached to me in varying degrees of familiarity and with varying reactions of trust or distrust. My own feelings became ones of affection and protection, sometimes amusement, sometimes dismay, always curiosity as to what was to happen next. I visited them at all hours of the day, and for a number of nights slept on the ground in the most active area so that I could find out something of their night behavior.

This western spotted species was discovered over a century ago, in 1858, by Xantus at Fort Tejon in southern California, but not found again until 1872 when Charles Bendire saw one near Tucson, Arizona. Since then, whatever rediscoveries may have taken place, the species has been considered a rare one, and nothing, so far as I have been able to find, has been chronicled of their lives during a full nesting season. The owls are ordinarily nocturnal, not easily disturbed when on their daytime roosts, and so retiring of nature that they seek deeply shaded canyons and forests along the Pacific coastal belt or inland mountains, characteristics that make the mere sight of one a notable event.

My notable series of events began with the woodland encounter of a well-camouflaged pair of these rare relatives of the eastern Barred Owl, and continued through observations of five broods, ranging in size from one to three. In two of the seven years I watched them, no nesting took place. The pair I first saw, resident parents throughout these years, were perched side by side about twenty feet above the ground and were running their bills through each other's neck feathers, an action I have since seen mother and owlets use. Possibly feathers so located need assistance in cleaning. Or maybe it is the owl version of a caress. Certainly one might call it "necking."

Now and then during the winter, after much searching, I was able to locate one of the owls, never two at a time, perched quietly during the day under the shelter of heavily leafed trees, so I knew they were resident in the area. And in the spring I discovered a nest high in the fork of a pine tree, above a thick tangle of brush and fallen limbs. It was evidently the abandoned nest of Red-tailed Hawks, one of a number in the vicinity. Within this home three hungry owlets were hatched, and from it their voluntary descent was miraculously accomplished without harm, even though they could not yet fly.

They were appealing young creatures, but comical in appearance and behavior, covered with gray down and with stubs of tails like those of cottontail rabbits. They had baby-blue eyes and trusting dispositions, and aside from food their central objective in life those first days out of the nest was to *climb*. When hawks leave a nest volun-

Out of the nest but still unable to fly,
two little Spotted Owls busily hop about the forest floor (above)
preparatory to climbing back up their tree
and perching companionably on a branch (right)

tarily they can fly a short distance, but these owls had not yet attained that ability. And yet, instinctively, their first reaction was to get off the ground at once, and back into the shelter of the trees. So, with grasping talons and stubby wings flapping wildly, they *climbed*, inch by inch, whatever tree was nearest, in a prodigious effort to escape the perils that threatened them below.

One rainy evening, their down feathers tightly curled like the fur of a gray Persian lamb coat, they hopped from branch to branch, sometimes falling to the ground and hopping along again among the twigs and leaves. When this happened, climbing must again be attempted. Pine trunks are rough, and with flapping wings and clinging talons a floundering climb of fifteen or twenty feet can be negotiated, although with difficulty. But this time one owlet fell near a tree with a smooth trunk, and it took him many minutes and furious effort to reach its first branch, only about two feet above ground. During this struggle I was agonizing right along with him, and offered him a stick as perch so that I could lift him to the desired stub. He distrusted my intentions and angrily clacked his beak at me. (In a later year I reacted to a similar situation by putting on heavy gloves and lifting the traveler to a safer place.) At this, the male adult flew in and gave me the only scolding ever received from either parent. The young owl finally made it, and the next night was high in a tree with the two others.

Two of the young habitually perched side by side, the third and smallest one, perhaps a male, either by himself or beside the female parent. A two-and-one segregation was also seen when owlets were in the nest, two on one side of the female, the third on the other. On one of the occasions when all three were found together, this time perched in line on a hazelnut branch, they were photographed. These three managed to survive the perils of the ground and any others between them and adulthood. But in another year, when two owlets were hatched, one was taken by a predator, perhaps bobcat, fox, raccoon, or skunk, in its third night near the ground. A pitiful trail of feathers led away uphill from the perch of the previous day.

As with other birds, there seems to be a ritual surrounding much of their behavior, and mating is usually one of the most ritualistic of behaviors. So I felt it was with the Spotted Owls, though my opportunity to observe was limited both by rough and brushy terrain, and by darkness. However, on a number of evenings between the time of the owls' awakening and darkness, I did note that copulation was preceded by a certain series of procedures. A rather noisy flying around was the first step. At this time the seldom-used loud "cau-cau" call was uttered. Finally, the male changed perches and copulation took place quite quickly. The female remained on this perch, whistling, while he flew off, usually calling from the middle distance with a succession of single notes. I saw this happen twice in one evening. At another time it occurred on a series of evenings between March thirteenth and twenty-ninth, and in this year the female was on the nest by April first. Only one owlet came from the nest that year. At another time I was interested to note that while this courtship was going on, a pair of Horned Owls was dueting quite audibly in the middle distance.

Early one March of a later year when seeking the owls, I began to hear calls and more of the whistles than usual, and soon realized that two owls were involved. The next night I saw the two perched near each other on different branches of the same tree. As dusk approached they got livelier, moving their heads and changing their perches. Not until it was nearly dark did they start to call and whistle, and then there was much chatter between them. About a week later they were evidently courting. A photograph taken at this time shows one of the owls on a pine stub looking, shall we say "adoringly"?, up to the perch of the other about twenty feet away. This evening was an active and noisy one, there being many calls and whistles and much flying around together.

By mid-March only one bird was in evidence, so the female had evidently started incubation. Calls were less frequent, but some came from the direction of what I later knew was the nest. It was in early April that I located the round head and the tail of the female visible above the rim of a Red-tailed Hawk's nest in the top of a pine tree. I was able to watch her comings and goings without too much difficulty. The male spent his day hours nearer his hunting spots, not by the nest, but at evening he reported for duty, usually carrying on a brief conversation before he left for the night's job.

The female was very faithful to her responsibilities, leaving the nest only for very brief intervals, not more than ten or fifteen minutes at a time. One evening she left at 6:55 for some nearby trees. The male went to the nest at 7:10, and, not finding her on the job, called with an angry succession of notes, keeping this up (she, meanwhile, answering with whistles) until she returned, when he left at once. Since, four days later, I saw food taken there for the first time, it may have been that the male had taken food to newly hatched young, and his angry notes were calls to the female to come tend to her feeding job, one he did not feel was his responsibility.

With precise aerodynamic control,
a Spotted plunges to earth and seizes a rat

Late in April I first saw the white downy body of one of the three young, and from that time on until they left the nest late in May, I had frequent glimpses of their white heads and dark-rimmed blue eyes peering over the edge.

The male kept union hours, hunting and helping only during the night, even when the female was hunting at any time of day or night. He received his pay by eating the heads of the rodents he caught before delivering them as food for the young. As decapitation of prey caught by the female was also customary procedure it may be that head bones are too large for the young to swallow. It was always the female who tore the prizes to bits and fed the owlets. While the young were still in the nest there was a definite ritual in the exchange of food from male to female. This took place in a nearby tree to which he called her, and was preceded and accompanied by long vocal consultations between the parents.

One evening in May the ritual varied. Evidently the hunting had been poor, and by 8:30 the male had brought nothing to his family. He came to a nearby pine, calling and whistling several times. The female, who was in the nest, did not leave it or answer as usual. She did not mistake his story as a call to get food. It appeared that he was unsuccessful and was telling her about his bad luck, and in about fifteen minutes he flew away again. The whistle call used at this time was a rare one for him, but a common call for the female.

Later, when the young were out of the nest and perched in trees nearby, the male still took his catch to the female, who, in turn, tore the headless mouse or rat to pieces and offered it in her beak, closing her eyes meanwhile (for protection from hungry children?) as she tenderly and gently but very persistently offered tidbits. If the male, on arrival with food offerings, found that she was not nearby, he sometimes gave a young one the rodent to deal with as best it could. This "best" was often very poor. There was a technique to tearing the animal apart that the young had not yet mastered. An ear is first torn off, to break the resistant skin, then the spinal column broken by a quick twist of the beak, the head eaten by the adult and the remainder torn apart to be given as food to the waiting young. Often intestines are discarded, though not always, and of course they are swallowed as part of the whole animal when that is taken as one huge swallow. Still later, when the young were nearer adult development, whole animals of small size were given to the young by the female to be swallowed by them, head-end always first.

Rarely was the game taken any larger than wood rats. On one occasion I found a young owl struggling to cast a pellet, that neat little package of indigestible fur and bones that is regurgitated by owls as by other birds that eat the whole skeleton of prey, be they hawks, kingfishers, flycatchers, or shore birds—these from my personal observation. For a full hour and a half the young owl twisted and turned and shook his head violently, to no avail, meanwhile holding something in his talons that was long and gray. Exhausted, he dozed off for a while, then flew to another branch and again struggled with the pellet, even clawing at his open beak in his efforts. He finally dropped from his talons the long gray leg, complete with foot, of a tree squirrel. Finally he clawed from his throat not a pellet, but the other long leg bone of the squirrel, which had been stuck there for over ninety minutes.

It has been emphasized by other writers that the Spotted Owl is extremely nocturnal. I did not find this so with the female when under the stress of providing for three fast-growing fledglings. During the year of the triplets she hunted at any hour of the day or night, and her only sleep must have been catnaps between hunting expeditions. The male quit at dawn, usually heralding this retirement with a last bit of conversation before going to his daytime perch. When there he evidently kept in touch with what was going on, for even in midday a single call from him let them know where he was. And I had two encounters with him during the day, which I'll describe later.

It was during this nesting that the female became sufficiently trusting to accept proffered food, which I started by releasing live mice from a cage. At the sight of the first one, from her position in the nest, her large round head rose above the edge, dark eyes opening from sleepy slits to huge, brown disks, and she launched herself silently from the nest to seize this prize.

Her flight never failed to thrill me. Completely silent except when her feathers were wet from bathing, she negotiated narrow passages between tree limbs as if flying where room was infinite. Since her wingspread must have measured several feet, such accuracy and dexterity seem remarkable.

Both birds were skilled hunters, but not infallible. Many times they made "dry runs," missing the intended prey. But what about the many marvelous catches that seemed so easy, but were in heavy growth, or prey colored like the dead leaves on the ground? It was not just eyesight that was used to locate food. I once saw the owl fly out over tall grass from a low perch about two and a half feet from the ground for a distance of about thirty-five feet and pounce on a mouse that he certainly could not have seen unless the minuscule waving of the grass stems guided him. And on another occasion in a neighboring meadow one flew from a small pine tree across a stretch of grass, around the ground-hugging limbs of a fallen tree, full forty-five paces, and caught a mouse in an area he could not even have seen from his perch. To super-acute hearing must surely go the credit.

When the young had been out of the nest about three weeks I noted a difference in the feeding ritual. The female no longer whistled to the male as before when she felt it was time for him to wake up and hunt. And he no longer called to her when food was caught, and no longer brought it to her to feed to the young. Instead he took his catch directly to one of the latter, something done before only when Mama was busy with a catch of her own. And when another week had passed, the owlets became noticeably alert to any sound on the ground and started practice landings and take-offs by repeatedly flying down from low perches, sometimes walking a few steps among the leaves, then going up again to another branch. Now flying eighty to a hundred feet easily enough, but often with feet dangling, they did not always fly toward the mother as before, but rather back and forth near her. She still tore the catch apart, feeding it in bits to them, still eating the head first. When all but the tail end was eaten on one catch she called the unfed baby to her with the low murmuring feeding talk. Except for this, a whistle now and then, and the hissing hunger call of young, they had become nearly silent.

The next step in their development was an exercise in practice pouncing techniques, quite amusing to watch. A given area near the base of a large tree seemed to be the favored spot, and if I happened to be sitting there, no matter to Junior! He would come down, waddle around on his fuzzy legs, and—boom!—pounce on a leaf a few inches below him with both feet, sometimes nibbling at the leaf afterwards. If I rustled the leaves with a stick the young owls were at once interested, and several times came to the ground to investigate, sometimes landing, sometimes circling and flying back again. In the daytime I have seen them tear leaves to bits, holding the twig in talons as if it were a mouse. In particular the yet unfed young do this when another has already been fed, as if playing a neglected child in a game of "Let's pretend." One of them had a startling experience in late June. A brittle branch broke under him, and he fell some feet before he could make his wings take hold. In so doing he caught his talons in the twigs of a dead limb, and for a number of seconds, perhaps twenty, hung by his feet, upside down, then freed himself and flew away. (I once saw a young Osprey on his first flight from the nest have a like experience.)

After the female had accepted gifts of live mice, and then dead ones for her young, I tried an experiment one mid-afternoon just to see what would happen. I brought with me a rubber rat, such as dime stores sell for animals' toys, placed it on the horizontal limb of a tree, and wiggled it around in the attempt to make it look alive. The female was sitting on the same limb about fifteen feet from me. She watched closely as I held it by the tail and pushed it back and forth, but did not come for it with her usual ungainly parrot-like pigeon-toed walk down the limb. Suddenly, from behind me, there was a rush of wings, and the unseen male swooped past my shoulder, grabbed the rubber toy from my fingers with his talons without touching me at all, and flew with it to a nearby tree. The female followed him; there was the usual exchange-of-food talk, and she then took the rat to a low pine stub branch, but accidentally dropped it on the ground as she landed. Meanwhile I had been worrying about what rubber might do to an owl's stomach, so I hastened to retrieve the rubber toy. For three quarters of an hour after that she searched diligently for the lost prize, evidently not having judged it by odor or texture to be an imitation of what she had taken it to be. She went from limb to limb, to bushes, and down to the ground, then back again, returning a number of times to the place where the rat had fallen, giving her low whistle call as she did so. Finally she gave up and searched no more. This behavior was in seeming contradiction to another pattern I have observed. When a piece of rodent that was being torn up has at times dropped to the ground, there was no effort to find and retrieve it. This loss of the whole animal may have been confused with the ability of live prey to escape and hide.

At another time, after the female had caught a live rat and taken it up to a tree limb, she dropped this one also. She did not go down to it at once, but the male appeared and seemed very interested in it as he perched above the spot. (Both this occurrence and the one with the rubber rat took place in the afternoon. The male was not so far away or so fast asleep as one would have thought from his lack of bringing in provisions.) She warned him with a couple of whistles, and he left at once, returning to his former perch and seeming to pay no more attention to her activities. She caught the rat, ate the head and stored the body on the ground in a little hollow at the base of a tree, the only time I saw storage on the ground. (Pads of matted pine needles on pine limbs, or broad limbs themselves were often used as a pantry to store food for future use. And I had proof that stored food was later used, for a white rat that I had released and she had caught was brought out a day later and fed to the young.) Again Papa had evidently been more conscious of what was happening than he had let on, for after storage had been accomplished he flew to the spot, secured the carcass of the rat, and flew off with it!

Aside from the incident of the squirrel I have never had evidence of the owls' having caught prey other than small rodents. Once I offered a freshly dead mole, and although it was investigated, it was disdainfully and with unmistakable aversion refused. It remained in the same place until it disintegrated, evidently disliked by other animals of the woods as well as by the owl.

There are many other birds in these steep wooded valleys, small birds such as robins, which divebomb the owl when it has perched near their nests, Swainson's Thrushes, which sing their beautiful rising roll of song late into the evening, nesting Red-tailed Hawks, whose daytime cries are ending just about the time that the owls' calls begin, and many other birds, including other owls. Saw-whet and Screech Owls have been heard nearby, and the Great Horned Owl also nests in the vicinity, although one writer feels that the two are not to be found together, since the Horned may prey upon the Spotted. Their hunting territories must overlap in this particular area and I have never seen any conflict between the two species. Once, when the female was murmuring to an unfed baby, evidently calling it to come to her, a young Red-tailed Hawk heard the call and flew in. Instantly the young owls dropped down to low perches. The mother squatted on the tree limb in a defensive pose, ready for eventualities. The hawk caught sight of me, and flew away. Another time early in the morning, when trying to locate the owls, I heard a scolding note that I had credited to jays, a repeated single note. I found the young owl silently squatting on a horizontal limb, while a young Cooper's Hawk hopped around in a very agitated manner about twenty feet from the owl, running up and down the limb he was on, hopping from limb to limb, flying across to another one, then repeating the performance, at the same time constantly calling the single repeated "keh-keh-keh-keh." This call came in groups of four to eight notes, too fast to count singly but counting by groups I found that they ranged from about forty-three to sixty-seven notes, the group of eight usually ending

A mother Spotted with two chicks, well-fed (note rat tail protruding from the mouth of the one in the center) and safe. But three nights later the owlet at right was killed by a predator

with several extra "kehs." The young owl sat very quietly during the entire performance, not moving its head or calling until the hawk had flown away. Then the hawk returned, calling again, and, strangely, the owl flew *toward* him, causing his retreat. But his calls continued for some time. The owl sat, fluffed and quiet. This had taken about an hour. Whether the hawk's call was for food, so unlike the "Ko-*ree*-a" of the young Red-tail, I do not know, nor just what meaning was implied in the owl's changing reaction. No other hawk appeared or was heard.

There was a small brook at the bottom of the hill below the nesting area, and several times I have seen the female owl fly up the hill with wet feathers, noisily, to dry herself nearer home. One morning I was fortunate enough to watch her at her bath in a small pool surrounded by ferns; she was standing on a partially submerged log, with just her feet in the water. She dipped her beak in the water, then put her head in, first from one side and then the other, with a *rolling* motion, meanwhile beating her wings. When she flew away the sound of the wings was noticeable, quite unlike the silence of her usual flight.

Each year I have followed the feeding of the young until the owlets finally disappear to find territories of their own, but I have never heard them give an adult call, although they were fully clothed in adult feathers. The last bit of fuzzy, gray, immature plumage was a tiara-like area around the back of the head, and then it too changed to spotted brown feathers, and visually all the owls were alike. When the young could no longer be found, the adults also were elusive. Favorite perching spots were vacant, the woods silent of owl calls, the mice given a chance to multiply for the next year's nesting, and I felt at loose ends and lonesome. At this time of writing and for several years past they no longer seem to be in this long-used spot, nor have others taken over there. Man began to encroach upon it, but they seemed to have no fear of humans—too little fear, perhaps? Preying Horned Owls may also have decimated them—who can say?

The one supremely successful nesting from which three adult owls finally developed was followed the next year by a family of two owlets, one of which was killed soon after leaving the nest, as mentioned earlier. The third year there was no nesting, the fourth only one owlet came from the nest, falling onto a very open visible spot of ground. I was afraid of nighttime predators so lifted him and put him on as high a branch as I could reach. I found him in the same bush the next day. In the fifth year there were again two young owls. It is said that as many as four eggs may be hatched, but a family of three was the largest I witnessed, and it required such constant hunting to keep them fed, even in a year of plenty, that I wonder how four could be cared for satisfactorily.

The calls of the Spotted Owl are many and varied both in pattern and in pitch, one even sounding like a squeaking axle. In general the basic call is an alternation of long and short notes that sound somewhat like the barking of a small dog, though there is a nasal quality, almost ocarina-like, that is different. This call, consisting of a long note, a pause, two short notes, a pause, and then a final long note that descends at the end almost into a grunt, is the most frequently heard, especially from the male. He also uses a series of single notes, anywhere in number up to about thirty-two, gradually ascending in pitch and decreasing in speed toward the last of the call, also with a crescendo effect. I have heard this given in conversation with the female near the nest. Her answer, and her call usually, is what I choose to call a whistle, most easily imitated by humans on an indrawn breath. This, too, is rising in pitch and has a definite "push" or accent at the end accompanied in the bird by a noticeable jarring of the body as she achieves the accent. This whistle is capable of many variations in loudness, and probably of many meanings. It can be loud, but is more often soft and plaintive. It seems to be a mode of conversation, but is infrequently used by the male and *constantly* used as mother-to-child talk. The female whistles in the nest very softly and gently, a sound barely audible to a listener below the tree; she whistles when it is time for the male to bring in the evening dinner offering to the young, waiting in the nest or in tree branches after they have left the nest; she whistles in answer to his food call when he has a rodent to offer. But when she has food for the owlets and is taking it to them she uses a murmur in her throat that sounds much like the *wing* sounds of a flying Mourning Dove. I once heard a Great Gray Owl, high in an evergreen in Yosemite National Park, talk to himself with much the same kind of murmur, but louder. During the evenings when I thought that mating was taking place there were other calls, some of them harsher than those already mentioned. There is a "kak" sound, and one that might be written "caow!" During the night, from my nearby sleeping bag, I have several times heard loud calls like the explosive "Ouch!" of a child. The hunger call is like the hiss of escaping steam, but not loud and raucous like that of the Horned Owl. However, it brings results when persistently used. One night an insistent baby nearly got pushed off the end of a pine stub by his mother, who kept crowding him and shoving torn bits of mouse at him. Finally he climbed onto her back to save himself from a fall!

My family relationship with these successive broods consisted, from the owl point of view, mainly in my being the provider of special treats. For myself, the view of family life among them was of consuming interest. The interrelationship between the members of the family, the development of the young, who were so accustomed to my presence that they paid no attention to me, even coming down beside me to do their "pouncing" exercises on dead twigs and leaves, the division of labor between the parents—the male catching food but not feeding it to the young, nor incubating, the female hunting at any hour of day or night but the male only at night—the differences in dispositions of the young birds (one pair in particular was so rough with the mother in the demand for food that she fled from them rather than toward them with it, her ambivalence resulting in considerable confusion of purpose)—all this was rich reward for the time spent.

The female especially became a personality to me. She would come silently flying toward me through the trees when I arrived imitating her whistle. She often sat beside me for thirty minutes or so when not actively searching for food, and she several times perched on the toe of my boot, as I sat on the ground, almost too close to focus my camera. E-flash exposures by the dozen disturbed her not at all. I have stroked her soft feathers as she perched on a stubby pine limb, and fed her many pounds of meat chunks from my ungloved hand, with never a scratch resulting. So when in the eighth year of my acquaintance with the owls the male called in vain for his mate, and she seemed to have disappeared, and in the ninth was replaced by a female who did not know me, I could only hope that nothing I had done or said had caused her any harm or been a betrayal of that greatly valued and thrilling trust, the confidence of a creature of the wild.

MEASUREMENTS   Length 16½–19 inches; wingspread 45 inches.

VOICE   Spotted Owls are usually considered to be birds of heavily wooded country sometimes split by ravines and rocky canyons. As such their habitat is not conducive to human visitations after dark and few people have carried on twenty-four-hour-a-day observations into their homeland. As a result of inaccessibility many

A piece of horsemeat in her beak, a Spotted Owl
grips the toe of the photographer's boot

naturalists have heard their calls but aside from saying that they have a varied vocabulary and a call that resembles the barking of a dog, little has been reported. The delicate nuances and the meanings of the notes were practically unknown until Grace Miller made her study.

Many of the calls resemble those made by Barred Owls, which reside in the eastern states and up into Canada. Considering the close relationship of Barred and Spotted, such similarity is to be expected. The eight-hoot call usually credited to Barred Owls (uttered in two four-note groups) has a facsimile uttered by the Spotted. It consists of a long note—a pause—two short notes—a pause—and then a long one that ends gutturally. This is usually uttered by the male Spotted Owl. Another call used by both Barred and Spotted with but slight differences is a series of single hoots, with Spotted Owls giving up to thirty-two in number, which gradually ascend in pitch but decrease in spacings toward the end of the call. This is often used conversationally by the male with the female in the nest. Her answers are usually whistled. The Spotted Owls have also been known to utter a turkey-like gobble or chuckle. The murmur used by the female as she feeds the young or calls them to eat is, as Grace Miller described it, like the sound made by the wings of Mourning Doves in flight.

The "caw-caw" call is rarely used, and since it preceded copulation in Grace Miller's study I think that calls of passionate intent may be customary with many birds but have not yet been interpreted as such. Barn Owls, for instance, have a peculiar clicking note almost metallic in quality. Because Barn Owls are comparatively abundant near human homes, this note has been heard by many naturalists, with the vocalizers rarely seen because of darkness. On several occasions when I not only heard the call but was also able to watch the birds, mating followed. In the surprising medley of calls used by Long-eared Owls I vaguely remember a different pitch or change in tonal quality when they became romantic.

Although Spotted Owls are usually quiet birds during the actual nesting and throughout fall and winter, they, like the Barred, can be noisy. Such vocalizing, wherein almost all their calls are used indiscriminately, usually occurs when they are actually moving from place to place in a small section of woodland preceding the nesting season; some of the calls are uttered in flight, others when the owls are momentarily perched. When this happens the listener gets the impression of an owl convention when in reality the medley is the vocal output of a single excited pair.

With eyes tightly shut, a Spotted takes a chunk of horsemeat
from Grace Miller's fingertips

NESTING   Spotted Owls are not choosy about nesting sites. In fact their only prerequisite is seclusion, which can be afforded by dense woods, caverns, stick nests in trees that are well hidden by foliage, or hollow trunks. Pothole or cavern nests are usually used year after year, but the tree nests in Grace Miller's study had only a single-season occupancy. The hollow trunk situation is also the preferred home of their eastern Barred Owl cousins. If a preference is shown by the western Spotted, the birds seem to be partial to potholes in cliffs or even roomy caves on the sides of ravines. Most observers feel that the birds do not build their own nests but appropriate the deserted nest of a hawk or raven. Western ravens often nest in the indentations of cliffs, so possibly the Spotted Owl's preference for such sites is based on availability. If deserted raven or hawk nests are not available, Spotted Owls will lay their eggs on the bare dirt.

Like all owl eggs, those of the Spotted Owls are white; they are possibly a little more oval than those of Barred Owls. The shell is slightly granulated, not glossy. Most records indicate that two eggs are normal, three occasional, and four extremely unusual. Such a low reproduction rate places them at the bottom of the list for egg clutch sizes for North American owls.

HOURS OF ACTIVITY   Although Spotted Owls are generally considered to be strictly nocturnal, Grace Miller found that in the stress of catching food for three young the female often hunted from three p.m. on, and occasionally throughout the entire day. The male, however, was a stickler for normal working hours, going to roost at dawn and not to be seen foraging again until dusk. A few observers examining young or eggs in a nest see parent birds, recently scared off, return to perch fearlessly almost on the nest edge. Others disturbed at a nest have flown a short distance and then, seconds later, when perched on a limb, have continued their daytime slumber.

FOODS   A. K. Fisher's monumental volume was published late in the nineteenth century at a time when bird collecting, egg collecting, and stomach analysis were pursued by many tireless observers. Detailed results of the last occupation crammed the pages of his book for almost every bird of prey recognized at that time. But of the

Spotted Owl he says, "Little is known of the habits of this species and absolutely nothing of the food."

Three quarters of a century have passed since that publication refuted the so-called benefits of hawk-and-owl-bounties then in vogue, but Spotted Owl foods are still little known. Even A. C. Bent's volume says, "Rats and mice of various species seem to be the favorite prey of the spotted owl, wood rats *(Neotoma)*, white-footed mice *(Peromyscus)*, and the red tree-mouse *(Phenacomys)*, which forages in the forest trees. It also, probably, eats some chipmunks and other small squirrels, other small rodents, and a few birds." W. Leon Dawson mentions two records wherein the remains of Pygmy Owls were found in Spotted Owl stomachs. Such feeding on other smaller owls is a common occurrence with the eastern Barred Owl, so it is evidently a trait retained by this western cousin.

OF SPECIAL INTEREST   Since the Spotted Owl was first discovered by Xantus in 1858, four races have been described on the basis of being lighter, darker, or with smaller or lighter spots, but with so few specimens in existence, the exact race status of the birds is questionable and due for revision. To confuse the nomenclature still more, Harry C. Oberholser states that "our investigation has resulted, furthermore, in the interesting discovery that there are two well-marked color phases in *Strix occidentalis*, the lighter of which is of comparatively rare occurrence."

Great Gray Owl

10

GREAT GRAY OWLS

INTRODUCTION Although I have never met Al Oeming, I have been aware of his existence for many years. Husky to the point of being a Canadian Paul Bunyan, this man of purpose and intellect was well known to sports fans who followed the wrestling circuits—circuits wherein there was a give and take of bruises for the quick and "easy" money. Thus financed, he was able to build his now internationally famous game farm at Edmonton, Canada, and it is justifiably famous. At this writing, a birth announcement lists five baby musk ox. Few zoos in the world can boast of a single captive of this rare animal, and if they do, it probably came from Oeming's stock.

To see, to find—let alone rear—any of the world's endangered animals (and the musk ox is one of these) takes a dedication and persistence possessed by few people. The pages that follow, recounting his quest for Great Gray Owl material, which finally culminated in a 129-page thesis, show that persistence was a trait of his at an early age, even when he was a student and athlete at the University of Alberta.

Most of the factual information in this chapter is by Oeming: voice, nesting, hours of activity, and food have been taken directly from his prodigious thesis. His knowledge of Great Gray Owls makes me believe that he will be the last to ever make such a study, for the Great Gray Owls are on the road to rapid oblivion.

Note: The Great Gray Owl of Canada and the northern states is almost a facsimile of the Lapp Owl, which inhabits Siberia and Scandinavia. Since bad weather conditions in Alberta plagued Oeming's study, photographic excellence was almost impossible, so many of the photos illustrating his chapter on Great Gray Owls are of the Lapp Owl—the Scandinavian counterpart of the American form.

AL OEMING ON GREAT GRAY OWLS   Few ornithologists have ever seen Great Gray Owls and there is every indication that even fewer will be privileged to view these magnificent birds in future years. Less than a quarter of a century ago Great Grays were not uncommon in the wooded areas north of a line that roughly coincides with the Canadian border, but when the pelts of red squirrels became valuable the picture changed drastically. Almost overnight owls were condemned, for most trappers are easily prejudiced against any animal that rumor credits with taking what they wish to catch. The Grays, being tame and docile birds, became targets whenever seen.

Just when or what originally aroused my interest in Great Grays would be difficult to answer. It might have been my friendship with the late Archibald Henderson, the veteran zoologist who in the early part of the century knew more about Grays than any living man. It might have been nature photographer Ed Jones, who was always in quest of something different for his Audubon screen tours. Or perhaps it was just the bird's increasing rarity, caused by what I considered to be an unfair persecution, that created a challenge—a challenge I accepted when it came time to work on a thesis at the University of Alberta.

Four years and thousands of miles later, traversed by jeep, snowshoes, horses, canoe, and on foot, owl observations and research proved that the unfair persecution charge was vindicated. Ed and I had found two occupied nests, had obtained fourteen dead specimens from varied sources, and had had shipped to us four live birds. From pellet dissections, stomach examinations, and months of observations, we checked foods down to the minutest detail. But of the rumored red squirrels as Great Gray food items there was not a sign.

As optimistic neophytes on this species of bird, Jones and I commenced our search in the spring of 1952 but little did we realize how tough an assignment we were undertaking. Snow was still on the ground, for it was early March, a period according

Al Oeming holds two 16-day-old Great Gray chicks

to Henderson's notes when the owls would be selecting their homes for the raising of young. Weeks passed as we tramped the woods and interviewed veteran trappers, lumbermen, and settlers. We scrutinized every Red-tail or goshawk nest to be seen in the hope that a Great Gray head would be looking over the edge. To say that we were disheartened would have been the understatement of the year. The only encouragement, which in itself was tainted with sadness, was the receipt of two dead owls from remote spots in Alberta, for even though these carcasses dropped the population by two more, they showed that some birds still existed. Maybe there would be better luck next year.

But 1953 was essentially the same: more dead birds, hundreds of tedious miles traveled—but not a live Great Gray to be seen. We had now used every mode of land conveyance known, through some of the toughest country in Alberta. After a discouraging ten thousand nonproductive miles, the thought struck us that the trappers, settlers, and rural school children might not shoot the birds if they were better informed, and might even become helpful assistants in our quest with proper information at their disposal. So the idea of printing a small illustrated booklet on the Great Gray Owl was conceived.

That fall five thousand brochures were circulated through the province, one to every trapper, logger, and northern school division. Farm and rural weeklies throughout the dominion carried the story of our search and the kind of information that was wanted. The Toronto *Star Weekly* had a striking picture with an accompanying article. Then we waited to see if the old adage "It pays to advertise" would pay off when the object was not only an owl but one that seemed on the verge of extinction.

Although the response to the booklet was most gratifying, bringing in at least seven records for Barred Owls where only two for the province had existed before, weather then became our enemy. The spring of 1954 broke all existing records for lateness and severity. Twenty below zero weather persisted until the end of April, and even May was extremely cold. Heavy falls of snow made traveling a veritable nightmare and if winter did not relent, and soon, it would be utterly impossible to gain access to the few locations where Great Grays had been reported.

Curtailment of our freedom of movement caused us to temporarily abandon distant trips, but one spot, the Corbett Creek country, was still available. In our first-year search this area had impressed us as ideal habitat for Great Grays. For miles around there was a growth of gigantic white poplar, and one of the two dead owls we had received had come from that general locality. Accordingly we made it our goal for the 1954 season and on our first day in the region two loggers cutting lumber informed us that a large "moon-faced" owl without horns or tufts had been seen some miles from their camp.

Eager and encouraged — but not overly so because we had gotten such reports before — we obtained horses from the logging camp and began riding in a twenty-five-mile arc through the best and likeliest patches of woodland. But after two days of plodding through the still deep snows of early April, tiring for both horses and riders, our hopes were definitely deflated as we settled into our sleeping bags.

The third day started as had the others — beautiful country — ideal for owls according to the books and notes we had almost memorized word for word. But, as was remarked just before crossing a large muskeg, "owls can't read." I was leading Ed by about a hundred yards when a hundred feet in front of me I saw a long-sought-for Great Gray Owl, perched on the thin tip of a dead tamarack. After two years and well over ten thousand miles of searching, the thrill couldn't have been exceeded if the bird had been a Dodo, a Great Auk, or even a dinosaur. Within a few minutes careful stalking narrowed the distance to twenty feet, which was good photographic range, and it also showed us why such tame and trusting owls were decreasing to the point of endangering the species.

The bird was hunting and we assumed it to be the male, which at any moment might catch a mouse and lead us in the general direction of mate and nest. We waited patiently, watching his every move and following his flight from perch to perch. And these flights in particular held our attention. They were slow, measured and soft, giving the bird an eerie wraith-like appearance as he glided through the great shadowy trees. Although dusk was imminent, if he had been "as blind as an owl," as the story goes, the lingering light would have had him crashing into twigs and branches — for his wings were huge billowing sails. They were of such size as to seem clumsy for life in a dense forest, but he missed branches by a fraction of an inch, making skillful use of this equipment evolved through the ages. Enormous for the pigeon size of his body, his wings render him outwardly, but not by weight, the largest of North American owls.

We were still elated when, the next day, we started to retrace our steps but decided to first recheck an old Red-tailed Hawk nest in a black poplar even though it had shown no signs of habitation when first found. From beneath we scanned it with glasses but saw no owls, so again we headed back to the heavy timber where our only owl to date had been watched. Two hundred yards from the nest we had just left, Ed stopped, dismounted, and gave an excited shout. There on the edge of a small grass clearing were the remains of a female Great Gray, recently killed by some other bird of prey. Evidence showed it to be the work of a Horned Owl, a bird heavier in weight but smaller in over-all size. Horned Owls, which have sub-specific relatives all over North America, in the Alberta region subsist to a great extent on snowshoe rabbits. This was a year, however, when the rabbits were at a low point in their four- or five-year cycle, and being hard-pressed for food Horned Owls were ready, willing, and well enough equipped to tackle almost anything.

So, again, we were discouraged. Our spirits had been manipulated as though on a yo-yo, up-and-down up-and-down. How we wished that the string would tangle in the up position! Just to make sure that this area had yielded all it could of findings, I climbed the tree. Within the nest there were breast feathers of a Great Gray Owl. Since it was late in the season, we presumed she had been incubating eggs that, without her protection, had been removed by some egg-eating animal.

Home again, we commenced to plan next year's attack on the Canadian wilderness, feeling that too much of 1954 had slipped by to make a comprehensive study of the birds. On May fourth, however, we received a letter from two lumbermen near Edson, about 140 miles west of Edmonton, who described a pair of owls resembling the picture of the Great Gray in our booklet. They stated that the owls appeared not in the least frightened by the presence of man and always hung about the same muskeg. It sounded too good to pass up and as it might be the break we were waiting for, we pressed on to investigate, despite foul weather.

From the loggers' residence it was a good six-mile trek as the raven flies, to the edge of a huge muskeg where the owls had frequently been seen during the past two weeks. A thaw made this travel as tough as any we had experienced. With each step a foot would stick in the mud and before another step could be made the mired foot had to be forcibly pulled free. But the loggers' story had been so good, so authentic-sounding in every detail, that we carried with us all the cameras and camping equipment that it was possible for two men to transport. The realization that, should the owls be there, each future trip over the ever-softening muskeg would be an increasingly difficult endurance test, was not a pleasant thought.

Arriving at the poplar woods fringing the muskeg, I started to look for an old nest that might be the home of our elusive subjects when a call from Ed Jones, his binoculars raised, made me join him. This was it, an unforgettable moment—our first Great Gray on a nest. Another could be heard hooting and calling from somewhere back of a nearby ridge.

Anxious to see what this home contained, I quickly put on my climbing irons and made the forty-five-foot climb. The female flew off and perched a scant ten yards away as I ascended and looked in on her two young, which were about ten days old. I mentally hoped that the yo-yo of our emotions had reached and would remain at the top. Ed and I immediately set up camp and rushed construction of a photography platform, for it was evident that no blind was necessary for these docile birds.

The female didn't waste any time returning to her young, for the weather was still extremely chilly. Later, her intense hooting, unlike any owl sound we had ever heard, caused us to rush forth from our tent in time to see the male deliver a mouse. He waited only long enough for her to take it from his bill and then quickly disappeared through the tall trees to continue hunting. This occasional persistent hooting of the female throughout the night told us when she was receiving a visit from her dutiful husband, and he usually carried a red-backed mouse—a mammal common to the big woods. At other times both by day and by night the female would repeatedly emit a low plaintive sound, like the soft cooing of a dove. We bivouacked beside this nest for three days, getting things arranged so that everything would be handy for our planned weekly visits.

It was with much reluctance that we left the huge birds, for in a few short days they had captivated us as personalities, symbolic of the quiet grandeur and majesty of these virgin woods. Unsuspicious in spite of our presence, they seemed unique to us, and we were getting a wealth of original information on behavior and diet. When evening came the woods were quiet except for the cooing of the female and the long-drawn hoot of the male as he continued his forays in the adjoining muskeg.

The day we arrived back in Edmonton, still elated about our find in the Edson area, a call came from a trapper at Rocky Mountain House about 160 miles southwest. The trapper's description of the owls he had observed was so accurate as to leave no doubt that they were the birds we sought. So again our road-weary jeep was hastily packed and we headed off once more. The trapper's cabin was actually fifty miles west

of Rocky Mountain House and twelve miles into the bush from the last passable road. All bush roads were tough going during this unusually wet year and we were constantly forced to winch out of deep holes and ford streams, swollen mightily with heavy rains that washed out the bridges. After a day of battling mud and water we arrived at the patch of timber where the birds had been seen two days before, and two hours later we spotted a hawk's nest. Sitting on the edge was our second female Great Gray.

In everything but temperament this pair resembled the Edson birds. Their plumage, their nest, their manner of flight, and their calls were similar. But instead of sitting placidly as I examined the two young, the female made constant dives at me, missing my head by only a bare six inches. And the males of the two nests were also different, for while the male of the Edson pair was very solicitous of his mate, remaining in almost constant attendance, this one made only brief appearances and was seemingly out of hearing range for longer periods of time. If these four birds had been study skins in a museum collection they would have been as alike as peas in a pod, but as living birds they were four separate temperaments, and if each had been studied separately there could have been four different conclusions drawn on the behavior of Great Grays.

From then on weekly trips to both nests kept us extremely busy, not only in actual travel to and from the nest sites but back at home trying to tabulate and make sense of the data gathered on each visit. Each week there were seventeen different measurements made of the owlets. Pellets collected had to be examined with the help of University of Alberta mammalogists to determine diet. Observations had to be logged in proper sequence; films developed, dated, and filed; and then there was the jeep. Unprecedented rains didn't help it in the least. We were constantly forced to push fallen branches and sometimes trees out of the way. Minor repairs to the vehicle, which was being taxed by us beyond the point of our being sane and sensible, took time we did not have. Even a black bear got into the act, breaking into camp and tearing sleeping bags and foodstuffs to shreds. Two hours after discovering his depredations, and two hundred yards from camp, I found my camera where he had dropped it after deciding that the leather case was unpalatable. Toothmarks on that case still remind me of my quest for Great Gray Owls.

The young birds were growing rapidly and by the second week in June had left the nest and were already over a mile from their homes, led into the vast muskegs by

Forty-five feet up in a Canadian poplar forest,
a Great Gray nest with two owlets

A soaring Lapp Owl,
European counterpart
of the Great Gray Owl,
about to attack photographer

their parents. At this vulnerable stage in their lives the birds remained very quiet and we could locate the young owls only by emitting noises in imitation of the adult birds and then listening carefully for juvenile answers. By the end of the third week in June the young were still farther from the nest and making short flights on their own. At this time the young birds were banded, for although we were going to come back again we felt that this might be our last chance. Both areas were visited a week later but no trace of parents or young was found. Although we combed the dense growth of spruce and pines of the Alberta muskegs, which extend for miles and miles, it was a futile search. Our Great Gray activities were now concluded for that year, but 1955 would see us looking for more experiences with these great birds.

Has the Great Gray a chance? This was a question we constantly asked ourselves. Having lived with the birds for over six weeks, we readily appreciated the difficulties they would have to face in Canada's booming Alberta. Great oil discoveries through-out the entire province were then already opening up vast tracts of virgin territory. Settlement is now pushing into new areas. Acre after acre of forest is being leveled by fleets of bulldozers. Pulp mills are leasing colossal holdings in some of Alberta's best bush lands. All this means less and less secluded wilderness, and only in secluded wilderness will the Great Gray live and breed. The birds sense no danger from intruding humans and can be approached at all times within a few feet. Such large conspicuous owls are too tempting for most of the trigger-happy invaders of the wilderness.

There is one hopeful sign at long last. The Alberta government passed an act protecting all hawks and owls in the province. It offers these great birds a possibility of survival. Forceful education and strict observance of the new law, together with the preservation of enough suitable nesting areas, may insure the ornithological world of the continued existence of one of its aesthetically most irreplaceable and economically beneficial species.

MEASUREMENTS   Length 24–33 inches; wingspread 54–60 inches.

VOICE   Until Oeming's study, comparatively little was known about the voice utterances of Great Gray Owls. Much of the owls' northern range was virtually unexplored at the time when they were considered common birds, and now that it is teeming with humans the birds are almost gone.

Unafraid, a Great Gray
looks sidelong at the camera

Archibald Henderson (1923) says of the notes of this owl: "A rather musical whistle was uttered frequently like oo-ih, sometimes very softly, and at others quite loudly. They also hooted several times, a deep booming Who-oo-oo-oo." Several authors have referred to the voice of this owl as a tremulous vibrating note, somewhat resembling that of a Screech Owl (A. C. Bent). This call, first reported by Charles Bendire in 1892 and credited to "some authors," has never been heard by Henderson, Randall, or Oeming.

From Oeming's thesis: "During the breeding season the male emits a very long-drawn call which lacks the depth and throatiness of the common Great Horned Owls. The female's response is always a shorter and somewhat screechier note and again bears no resemblance to the deep hooting of the Horned Owl. Henderson (1923) was the first to draw attention to the remarkable differences in the quality of sounds produced by the Great Gray Owl and the Great Horned Owl.

"In the following list the various notes the owls utter and the circumstances under which each call is given are described. The adult female has three definite calls: (1) A soft, dove-like 'ooh-ah,' at times very weak and more like a coo than a hoot. The sound is not loud and carries no great distance, usually tapering to a high raspy note at the end. It is repeated at irregular intervals throughout the day when the bird sits on the nest or perches in adjacent trees. (2) An excited, intense hooting like 'ooh-uh' repeated quickly and loudly. This was the signal that the male was arriving with food, and she would immediately begin to hunch on the nest and continue to call until she had taken the food from him. (3) A fast repeated but faint 'who-who-who-who,' uttered by the female when assuming a defensive attitude. This note and attitude have also been recorded in captive birds when alarmed by people or cats prowling nearby.

"The adult male calls are as follows: (1) A long-drawn hoot rather like a whistle, 'who-oo-oo' uttered near the nest, and often heard when the male could not be seen. It was often emitted when the bird was hunting in the muskeg. (2) A steady rumbling or pumping noise like 'oom-ah, oom-ah,' repeated for a minute or two and then started again whenever the male came close to the nest and the young were being handled. The throat of the male could be observed to maintain a pump-like motion and the beak appeared not to open. (3) A screechy whistle-like 'ee-ah, eee-ah' has been recorded only from captive birds and is uttered at any time throughout the day, most frequently in the spring and summer.

Lapp Owl and young

"Calls of the young: When still in the nest, the young would emit a very raspy screech, appearing to indicate hunger. These sounds would subside as the young were being fed and give way to a soft chirp-like utterance. A much louder, screech-like noise, 'ee-ih,' was emitted by the young after they had left the nest. An imitation of this sound proved the best way to locate the adults after the young had entered the hunting muskeg."

NESTING   The following is from Oeming's thesis: "In Alberta the most frequently chosen nesting territories appear to be the large white or black poplar woods. These poplar stands may be lightly mixed with either black spruce or jack pine. Nests are preferably near a sizable muskeg. These muskegs are characterized by a variable mixture of trees, shrubs, grasses, sedges, horse-tails, mosses and lichens. They conform in general to those described by Moss (1953), for northwestern Alberta. This is the hunting habitat for the male bird during the nesting period. Great tracts of these heavy poplar woods were once common throughout most of central and northern Alberta but are now chiefly confined to areas in the northwest and northern parts of the province. The typical Great Gray nesting woods are deep and secluded and well removed from agricultural activities."

Randall, Henderson, and Oeming believe this owl does not build its own nest but prefers to make use of those discarded by other raptors. In Alberta the species has made use of the nests previously occupied by Red-tailed Hawks, goshawks, Great Horned Owls, and occasionally crows. Twice Randall found the birds nesting on the top of an old spruce stump. And Oeming says: "Twenty-three nests found in Alberta were in the following locations, with the height indicated in feet. Aspen poplar: 45, 50, 40, 50, 35, 40, 45, 45, 45, 45, 80, 30, 50, 40, 45; tamarack: 50, 10; black spruce: 40, 25, 18; balsam poplar: 40, 30, 40.

"In the deciduous trees the site is usually in a crotch formed by two or three main branches. Other nests found in coniferous trees were in heavy branches near the trunk." The birds will frequently use nests in such flimsy and decrepit condition that the eggs are plainly visible from beneath. Neither Henderson nor Randall noticed any attempts by the birds to recondition the nests. A. C. Twomey (A. C. Bent) noted that one nest he discovered near Fawcett contained fresh tips of green pine needles and some newly added twigs. Oeming's personal observations agree with the findings of Henderson and Randall.

Oeming: "An accurate estimate of the nesting density of this species is extremely difficult to determine owing to the small number of nests located. The fact that the brochure circulated throughout northern Alberta revealed only two nests is some indication that this species does not have a heavy nesting density in the province. When one considers that trappers cover every square mile of Alberta's remaining wilderness at a time when the birds are most conspicuous and noisy, it may be assumed that the birds are, in fact, very scarce.

"The earliest Alberta record for a complete clutch of eggs is March twenty-third. The majority of nests have complete sets by the fifteenth of April. The number of eggs laid varies from two to five with three per clutch being the most common and two the next. Of the twenty-three nests for which records have been obtained, three contained five eggs, five had four eggs, nine contained three, and six, two eggs. The color is dull white and there appears to be no visible difference in this respect from the color of the eggs of other owls. The eggs are small for the size of the bird and are not as round as the eggs of most other owls, being between oval and elliptical oval in shape. The shell is not glossy but is rather roughly granulated. Measurements of twenty-four eggs from Alberta nests averaged 54.3 mm × 42.4 mm."

HOURS OF ACTIVITY

In most of the northern territory formerly occupied by Great Gray Owls it would be a difficult feat for them to be entirely nocturnal. Prolonged sunsets and early dawns in their areas, which are just south of the land of the midnight sun, would limit their activities to relatively few hours each night. The rare accounts of how nests have been found usually mention that the birds drew attention to the area by their calls in daylight as well as by night. This tends to show a twenty-four-hour activity, which is to be expected with most northern owls if Snowy and Short-eared Owls may be used as guides. Only the Hawk Owl of these northern species seems to be almost completely diurnal, but here again their rarity, which hampers observation, might be giving a false impression.

Oeming, in his Alberta study, says: "Great Gray Owls do most of their hunting, prior to the nesting season, in the late afternoon. Their activities during this period will only be sufficient to allay their own hunger, when prey will be eaten on the handiest stump. With the advent of the family, the male inevitably increases his hunting activities, he being the sole provider.

"During the first ten days of the life of the young owls the male is making rapid and frequent trips with food to the nest. A typical feeding schedule for a day during this period is as follows: 9:35 a.m., 10:30 a.m., 12:25 p.m., 12:45 p.m., 1:10 p.m., 2:10 p.m., 3:10 p.m., 4:10 p.m., and 4:30 p.m. A typical schedule for a day during the second week is as follows: 9:15 a.m., 11:30 a.m., 12:30 p.m., 5:30 p.m., and 5:50 p.m. During the third and fourth weeks the visits became less frequent, with not more than three trips per day recorded. The infrequency of daytime feeding despite numerous fresh pellets or castings suggested supplementary feeding by night. A typical schedule for a day during this period is as follows: 8 a.m., 11:30 a.m., 3:40 p.m. The fourth week's daily feeding schedule was more difficult to determine, for the young were away from the nest and continually shifting location. Night feeding was again indicated."

Of flight Oeming says: " . . . these birds are seen perched high on old tamarack stubs waiting to make a floating swoop at their prey. . . . The birds have been observed performing a gliding series of flights from stub to stub . . . occasionally stooping to pick up prey. . . . The flight is soft and measured and appears much slower than that of the great Horned Owls. . . . Their flight is not swift and the birds rely on accuracy of location and a noiseless approach rather than speed."

FOOD   Over a four-year period Oeming made a study of the stomach contents of all available Great Gray Owls collected in Alberta. Six of these contained twenty short-tailed meadow voles, none less than three and two had four; one had a dusky shrew; two had red-backed mice; one had a northern bog lemming. A. K. Fisher's report on nine owls, mainly from United States–Canadian border areas, gives about the same average of meadow voles, with a total of twenty-six. His examinations disclose that three of the owls contained five. In addition, one had a Brewer's mole; one a white-footed mouse; three had shrews; and one had a Snow Bunting. A. C. Bent reports that Dr. W. H. Hall took thirteen skulls of Redpolls from the crop of a single Great Gray and that Harry S. Swarth found the remains of an adult red squirrel in the stomach of one. A. C. Bent also reports that a wintering Great Gray in Massachusetts was seen with a partially eaten crow.

In Oeming's thesis he mentions that evidence of Spruce and Ruffed Grouse feathers near two nests studied suggests that if driven by hunger these owls can take larger quarry than usual. However, the assertion by Charles Bendire (1892) that Great Grays use snowshoe hares as their principal food was not backed by Oeming's Alberta study. Oeming also writes: " . . . although red squirrels abounded in both nesting areas, no evidence that they were being preyed upon came to light. Red squirrels are common throughout the range of the Great Gray Owl, but the evidence to date lends no support to the constant charge of the trapping fraternity that this species preys habitually on them."

OF SPECIAL INTEREST   Even though most of the evidence points to the fact that Great Grays are not especially migratory, there are occasional winter visitations several hundred miles south of their normal habitat. In theory, as with the periodic invasions of Snowy Owls, this movement is generally conceded to be caused by a food shortage in the north. Those that were not killed by humans on these early invasions usually disappeared by March and presumably returned to their northern homes.

However, a glance at the range map indicated breeding birds in Yosemite, first discovered by Joseph Grinnell and Tracy I. Storrer in 1915 and reported with regularity almost every year thereafter. This area is considerably farther south than any Great Gray habitat ever before reported. It may be that this population is a relic band left by the ice ages, but, if so, why only in California and not along the Rockies or eastern mountain ranges? Further observations may show a contiguous but spotty population along the west coast mountain range that ties to their normally northern habitat. Luckily their southern center of abundance is in a national park, where hunting for sport, I hope, will never come into vogue. With the rapid decrease of Great Grays where their residency is normal, it may well be that Yosemite at some time in the future will be their last stronghold.

In the case of Great Gray Owls, measurements are deceiving. They are considered to be North America's largest owl, but Snowy Owls and Horned Owls exceed them in both weight and strength, as the small size of the prey on the Great Gray's menu seems to prove. Just why an owl that lives in densely forested areas should evolve with an excess of extremely soft and over-sized feathers, when the Hawk Owl, which resides in similar habitat, is streamlined and compact, is anyone's guess.

Long-eared Owl and brood

11

LONG-EARED OWLS

A few miles from San Diego, California, there is a fairly deep ravine known as Tecolote Canyon. The name means "owl," probably handed down from the days of the early Spanish settlers. Differing from most of the landmarks named after animals, this canyon still contained a pair of owls when this study was made several decades ago.

It was beautiful, for the sides of the canyon were spotted with scrub oak and down at the bottom a small stream occasionally broke to the surface and watered a meandering line of stately sycamores. The owls lived in an abandoned Cooper's Hawk nest, about twenty-five feet from the ground. In the days when I watched the birds, the canyon enjoyed a strange but impermanent isolation, one that naturalists all over the country could, at that time, see near any city. It was too far to hike for the growing army that totes BB guns and .22's, killing and maiming anything that moves. Yet it was too close for the professional sportsmen, who prefer wilder areas, where they sometimes accomplish the same results. In time, the city will have blanketed this area. Perhaps ordinances and public feeling against slaughter will then give a certain protection to breeding stock if any remains.

The first time I climbed the scrub oak I almost reached the edge of the nest before there was any sign of life. Then from within came a low moan that rapidly intensified into a caterwauling remindful of a battle of angry cats. If I held my position the hideous noise would subside, but at my slightest movement it was instantly repeated.

Finally the face of a Long-eared Owl peered stealthily over the edge of the nest. Her pupils, contracted by the light to shoe-button size, stared into mine, which were possibly larger than normal, for I was only a foot away. After minutes of this eye-to-eye showdown I commenced to change position and climb higher. This rewarded me with one of the most beautiful sights I have ever seen in the wild. The female noiselessly extended her wings, raised the feathers to a vertical position and posed as a half circle of mottled mahogany. Although she probably weighed in the neighborhood of a pound, certainly not more, she stood her ground within arm's reach of me, bluffing with every ounce of her small being by assuming a position and size that I must admit was rather terrifying.

On my next visit the owls tried a different technique in their repertoire of many ruses. This time they became secretive and endeavored to blend into the background. One on a broken bough about forty feet from the nest unobtrusively watched my movements through eyelids closed to mere slits. Every feather was clamped to the body, which was held rigidly upright, giving the bird a stick-like appearance. The "ears" or feather horns from which this species derives its name were raised to vertical points until the over-all picture was of a rustic stump with two jagged splinters protruding from the top. While she watched, two-by-fours, plywood panels, and a seat were lifted to an adjoining branch without a movement from this living statue. Even when I left the partially constructed blind, the only hint of life was a slow turning of the head as I walked away.

Dusk brought another ruse, the highlight of the show. Now the actors seemed willing to try anything once as I put the finishing touches on the blind that was to hide me for many nights. First an anguished squeaking, like that of a small mammal in distress, drew my attention to a commotion in the grass. As I descended the tree and hurried to investigate, one of the owls flew up in the air only to alight again fifty feet farther on where another battle with an imaginary adversary was staged for my benefit. On and on the bird led me, and if owls have egos, hers was no doubt inflated as I followed willingly.

It was almost dark when I returned to the nest, but the persistent owls were far from through although their act now had to be watched in the beam of a flashlight.

Long-eared Owl raises wings in pose
used to intimidate predators

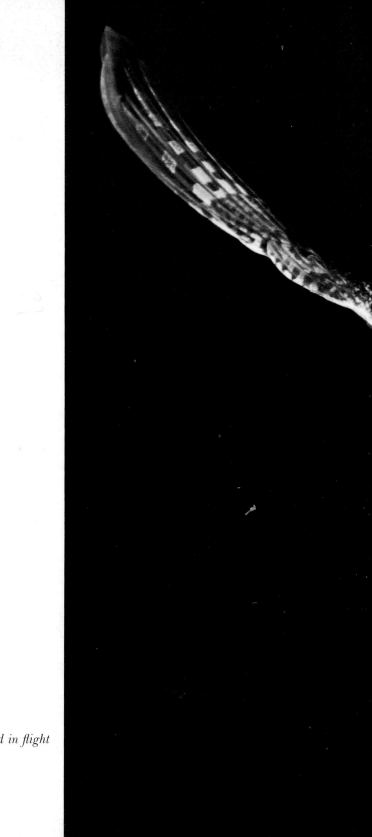

A Long-eared in flight

Lying on one side, an owl would push itself along the ground with a wing alternately flapping and dragging. It was the most brazen fraud I have ever witnessed, even better than that of the Killdeer — the supposed master of the feigned injury. If followed, the bird would lead me away, but whenever I retraced my steps toward the nest she miraculously recovered and flew back to intercept me on the path and repeat the antics. As long as the flashlight was pointed at her she would continue the convulsions, but if it were held a little to one side, she would veer around and actually seek the spotlight.

Repetition can make the best of pantomime tiresome and when I finally broke away to climb to the blind both owls became antagonistic. Every upward step from branch to branch invited dives, and the hurtling bodies of the birds missed me by mere inches. The tops of the scrub oaks formed an almost unbroken blanket of branches, twigs, and leaves, but the agile owls would dive through this maze at a breakneck speed and successfully navigate openings that seemed far too small for their speeding forms. The attacks of this night were purely a war of nerves, as evidenced by snapping beaks and low moans; but later in the study their dives out of nowhere were miraculously silent and really carried authority. After my head had been gashed a few times by raking talons, I came to the conclusion that safety was better than valor and thereafter I walked to and from the nest with a leafy branch held above me.

During daylight hours the young lay in a motionless heap, but with darkness they began to shift position and utter the rasping hiss of hunger. This call always started low and slow, as if vocal cords were being tested, but it rapidly increased in both volume and tempo until some sort of food was delivered by one of the adults. Even after they were satisfied with food, this rasping could still be heard, but, oddly enough, it then seemed to have a quality denoting contentment and was usually voiced by only one of the young while the others, gorged to fullness, slept in order to build more appetite for future meals. When the vocalizing one tired and snuggled into the pile, another would arouse enough to take up the call. During this period of inactivity each evening the call seemed to be used to mark or remind the adults of nest location, as if they didn't know!

This constant vocal advertising was unusual, especially when one considers that

A clutch of baby Long-eareds

most other birds try to keep a nest location secret. I had plenty of time to ponder this inconsistency while waiting for the feedings, generally scheduled to occur just after dark, again at about midnight, and just prior to dawn. Occasionally, in between swatting mosquitoes, I would stealthily take a long stick and disturb the young enough to quiet the monotonous call. Within several minutes an adult would appear, look over the situation, and then depart. This makes me feel that the call also denotes safety, security, or call it what you may, and that when it is stilled, the silence signals the parents that all is not well at the nest.

My first flashlight exposure produced immediate results, which I feared might bring a sudden end to these Tecolote Canyon observations. An adult had been standing over the young and glaring at the blind with its imposing array of reflectors and cameras. Finger pressure on the switch fired three bulbs simultaneously and for a fraction of a second the old bird froze with her wings outspread and then went off in full flight. For a hundred feet or more I could hear her breaking twigs as she blindly hurtled away to escape the noiseless man-made lightning.

For the next half hour the only noticeable sound was the constant hum of mosquitoes that ran a busy shuttle between owlets and photographer. During the construction of the blind, I had tested the strength of scrub oak. It didn't bend, break, or give and I visualized the bird as a disheveled mass of broken feathers and perhaps even shattered bones. But her navigation was flawless. I thought at the time that she must have radar equipment to have escaped the large branches, but evidently feathers equipped for almost noiseless flight rarely break when they mow down twigs.

Finally a plaintive mewing came from far down the canyon and it was answered by a subdued series of "who-o-os" from behind the blind. The young roused from their frozen positions and a moment later an adult perched on the edge of the nest. After this first scare, the adults seemed to consider the flash as only an unavoidable inconvenience, and in the many nights that followed they obviously lost all fear of having their pictures taken.

On my first visit the nest contained four young with enough difference in development to suppose that they, like the Barn Owls, do not delay setting until the clutch is completed. It also had one pipped egg and one infertile egg. The fifth infant, which hatched that night, remained the runt of the family for some time. Its develop-

Intimidation pose of Long-eared Owl

ment was slow and after about twenty days it disappeared entirely. Even though I felt that this was cannibalism, I searched for the puny one on the ground beneath the nest, but with no success. Later, when the other young reached the exploring age and began to hop from branch to branch, I found the missing carcass in the nest, picked clean and evidently devoured by brothers, sisters, and perhaps parents. Whether this bird had succumbed to attack or died naturally remains unanswered, but as I peruse my notes now and recollect that period in his life, I feel that mosquitoes might have had some bearing on his demise.

During early infancy the young were constantly brooded by their parents. If a face or a leg protruded from under the parental covering the mosquitoes would attack in swarms. But these attacks, when all the young were featherless, were divided. Sometimes one young would be a victim, and the next night another, but altogether they had ample time to heal. When the robust ones began to grow feathers—contemporary with the longer periods of desertion by the parents—the insects were seen to concentrate on exposed areas of featherless skin, particularly the feet or face. The runt was definitely retarded in this protective feathery growth and just before his disappearance bore the brunt of all insect attacks, which were formerly divided among five.

This study on the Long-eared Owls entailed nineteen visits that averaged about six hours each night. A small six-volt light was kept burning about twenty feet away, hence I was able to list accurately the foods brought in by the parents while I was in attendance. During this time they delivered 40 gophers, 10 wood rats, 23 pocket mice, and the partial, mangled remains of nine other unidentifiable mammals. Feathered prey was entirely missing.

Several years ago I revisited Tecolote. Most of the giant sycamores were no more—manicured out of existence in the name of progress—and other, less suitable trees had been planted to take their place. A few of the scrub oaks on almost vertical hillsides remained, but tacked on the trunk of one was a sign—BEWARE: RODENT POISON—showing that the canyon had become contaminated, probably beyond redemption. Any owl drawn by a rodent increase naturally catches the weak and infirm and seldom the healthiest individuals as prey, hence a reestablishment of predators becomes almost impossible, and the only answer is more poison—poison that once started can rarely be stopped.

MEASUREMENTS   Length 13 – 16 inches; wingspread 39 inches.

VOICE   From my observations at a number of Long-eared Owl nests, I believe that these owls have a vocabulary greater than that of all others. They seem to have a sound for every mood or circumstance, and in the case of nest disturbance freely switch from typical begging notes to outright profanity. Furthermore, if both of those fail, they will mimic other animals and even improvise a few sounds that seem to occur on the spur of the moment. In mimicry I have heard them almost duplicate the "whoo-who-who-whooo" of Horned Owls, the screech of Barn Owls, and possibly the quavering whistle of Screech Owls, although the latter call could have been the real thing, since Screech Owls occurred in the area and the Long-ears were out of sight at the time.

Notes of protest are a mellow series of three notes such as "wat-wat-wat" interspersed with low whistles and beak snapping. When I was attacked at night, each time an owl's talons hit my scalp this contact was accompanied by a carefully timed "waat." It was so similar to the call of a Western Gull when diving and protecting its eggs or young that even now — many years later — I expect talons to strike me when I hear the sound on gull islands.

Besides the calls already mentioned, Long-ears bark and whine like a litter of spoiled puppies. Sometimes when undisturbed they will start a series of ten to twenty evenly spaced low hoots that, just before cessation, rise in pitch. All these calls, however, along with many others, are seemingly uttered only near a nesting area. When at their winter roosts, which are often occupied by a score of these birds, Long-ears are virtually mute. One such roost was in the topmost branches of coniferous trees at Douglas Manor, Long Island. A friend of mine had a home immediately beneath, and despite the fact that he swept pellets from his driveway every morning, the birds never disclosed their location by calls.

NESTING   Oliver Davie, in *Nests and Eggs of North American Birds*, writes: "Various nesting places are selected; such as a hollow tree or stump, rift of rock, an old crow's or hawk's nest, which is repaired with a few sticks. In some localities the nest is made on the ground or on low bushes, and the same nest is occupied for several years." The nesting of present-day Long-ears is confined almost exclusively to the old stick nests of other birds, usually twenty feet or more from the ground. Although ground nesting and a hollow tree nest is mentioned by A. C. Bent, such homes are so exceptional for the birds I can't help but believe that Davie's casual "on the ground . . . rift of rock . . . hollow tree" is the result of a faulty identification of eggs and does not describe the typical sites, even in those days.

Most observers feel that the presence of nesting Long-eared Owls is vitally dependent on a certain amount of tree cover, and where wooded areas are abundant and widespread, the nesting pairs of owls will be found well spaced. However, there have been many instances of so-called nesting colonies, the sociability being due possibly to cleared areas surrounding a small forest and concentrating several pairs, or to the existence of several unused nests such as those left by a pair of Cooper's Hawks or even to those left by a rookery of herons.

Most owls known to be yearly residents of a territory will remain unless the breeders are killed or eliminated by some other cause. Long-ears, however, are undependable birds, often residing in a woodland for several years and then suddenly deserting the region for no apparent reason. Conversely, areas not known to have resident Long-ears will suddenly—almost overnight—sprout several pairs of the birds. An analogous desertion and sudden appearance in another area occurs with the rare White-tailed Kite found in California. With these diurnal birds, local fluctuation of mouse populations is usually given as the cause. Long-eared Owl movements might be motivated by a similar decline or abundance of mice, which are their primary food.

HOURS OF ACTIVITY
From my observations I believe Long-ears to be one of the most nocturnal of all the owls. I have never seen one fly until well after dusk unless forcibly driven from a roosting tree or prompted into action for the protection of eggs or young. However, as their nesting range extends northward into Canada, where nights are short, it might be that they are forced to do some flying without the cover of darkness. Circumstantial evidence of some strange but reliable food statistics where birds outnumbered rodents as food makes me wonder if there aren't some individuals that do not fit the norm, a few oddballs that almost had to do some daylight flying to catch the unusual prey reported.

FOOD A. K. Fisher details the foods of 107 Long-eared Owls, from all over the United States. The stomachs contained 87 mice, 3 shrews, 1 rabbit, and an unidentified small mammal. Of bird remains, the same stomachs contained 7 sparrows, a junco, a kinglet, a warbler, and a goldfinch. Of game birds, there was 1 quail. They also contained a few insects. Fisher examined about 50 pellets he collected and they disclosed the following foods: 95 meadow mice, 19 pine mice, 15 house mice, 5 white-footed mice, 3 Cooper's mice, 23 little short-tailed shrews, 3 short-tailed shrews, and 13 birds—of which 11 were sparrows, 1 a bluebird, and 1 a warbler.

Most reports show this same general menu is taken by the average Long-eared Owl, but there are some bizarre exceptions based on examination of pellets collected at two localities. Dr. Charles W. Townsend found in pellets that he collected 13 species of birds, totaling 23 individuals, as well as 4 species of mammals, totaling 25 individuals. Pellets collected by F. M. Jones contained the remains of 46 birds and 45 mammals. Although many naturalists feel that this taking of birds is seasonal and limited to the time that young are in the nest, my observations of well over a half dozen owl homes support just about the same ratio that Fisher found in stomach analysis. Until that 50 percent bird and 50 percent rodent ratio coming from only two separate owl roosts is substantiated by more studies, I prefer to think that such foods were the preference of individuals and do not necessarily apply to the species in general.

Short-eared Owl on the arctic coast

12

SHORT-EARED OWLS

Short-eared Owls are cosmopolitan, occurring on every continent in the world with the exception of Australia. As insular residents they are notable also, being the only native nocturnal land birds residing in the Hawaiian chain, the Galapagos, and some other far offshore islands. Their range in the Americas is stupendous, for they are found from Tierra del Fuego north to the arctic circle.

Holes in trees, old hawk nests, and cliff sides are typical homes for most owls, but the Short-eared, even where protective crannies are available, hide their nests only on one arctic island, Oomalashka, where they use burrows. Over the rest of their range they nest on the ground. Whereas most owls are shy about their romantic life and fulfill it in darkness, the Short-ears are largely diurnal and are not averse to displaying their love intentions while flying high in the air. Most owls, too, withhold a few secrets of their travels by flying at night, but Short-eared Owls, by their daylight activity, are an open book. We know that those of the far north occasionally wander in flocks and winter in temperate climes where mice are occurring in an abundant cycle.

My experiences with these interesting birds are spotty and inconclusive. The only study I started, on a pair found nesting on the Colorado prairie, was prematurely ended by a violent hailstorm that shattered the eggs. A colony I occasionally watched, but never with serious intentions, was completely eliminated when the marsh at Flushing, Long Island, was reclaimed for a world's fair. But even though destructive habitat changes in the name of progress bother me, that done on Long Island probably saved some of the birds by forcing them out to other areas. During the duck hunting season, a score or so pairs lived in the area before the fair but were subjected to constant bombardment by hunters, and after a weekend, three or four lifeless owl carcasses could be found where they had fallen.

This useless killing and crippling led me to a strange example of the devotion of one owl to another. Early one Monday morning the excited angry calls of marsh wrens, blackbirds, and a Brown Thrasher drew me to a thick clump of cattails. In the center of this cover was crouching a Short-eared Owl with a badly broken wing. Hoping to patch the wound but unable to take him at the time, I searched the area and found a dilapidated crab trap that I placed over him and then proceeded on my way. On my return three hours later, a healthy owl rose from the spot, made a dive at me, and then flew off. On top of the imprisoning cover the beheaded carcasses of a meadow mouse, a Norway rat, and a Red-winged Blackbird were laid out as food for the unfortunate bird within.

Feeding of an entrapped owl by another is not especially unusual, but in every other case I know of it has occurred in the nesting season or immediately afterward. Thus, by supposition, the providing was done by one member of an actively mated pair, or the imprisoned one could have been a fully plumaged immature owl, still cared for by parents. This early experience of mine, however, was at a season when family teamwork was supposed to be forgotten and marital ties were not to be resumed for several months.

Aside from my short Colorado study, which terminated almost before it was started, and the encounter mentioned above, my observations are all fragmentary in nature; even though I made several field trips with the New Jersey ornithologist Charles Urner, it would be impossible without months, or even years, of study to comprehend his great knowledge of the species. During Urner's lifetime he made copious notes, and any bibliography on Short-eared Owls will refer to him more often than to any other authority. It is largely on his work done in the days when New Jersey had vast, untouched marshes that the material in the rest of this chapter is based.

On the first of several trips I made with Urner, we met at a spot just outside Eliza-

Short-eared with a broken wing

beth, New Jersey, and in those days the towns of the area had visible boundaries. They were entities separated by spots of semi-wilderness. There was "breathing space" to which a city dweller could retreat. Some, tired of being cooped up in buildings, headed for the small patches of native trees, others to the coastal beaches, but Urner's domain—our destination—was a nearby marsh shunned by most people. Throughout the drive, during the walk, and later while pushing our way through cattails, I pumped him for information; and now with his notes and articles before me, that trip and several that followed stand out vividly in my mind.

By the time we neared the interior of this moist area I was a Short-eared Owl expert, I thought. And then off in the distance where a slight rise in the ground encouraged the growth of marsh grasses instead of cattails, we saw a large bird in circling flight. I blurted out, "Marsh Hawk!" and after receiving a scathing look from Urner, the difference in the flight of the two birds was called to my attention. I learned a lot that day, and one of the lessons was to make sure before venturing a guess that sounded like fact.

The owl circling in the distance seemed to confine its actions to an area of six or eight acres, and as we watched, Urner's tips on identification became apparent. First there was the head, which gave the effect of a blunt-nosed bomb with wings. The gracefulness and perfect proportioning so applicable to Marsh Hawks in flight was entirely missing in the owl. The effect of stubbiness was produced perhaps by the lack of streamlining at the front end, combined with the short tail on the other, or perhaps even by the wing beats, which were much more rapid than those of the harrier—there was a hurrying, which broke picturesque glides seemingly more often than necessary. In perfect light there are plumage differences that instantly separate these two competitors living in similar terrain. But at dusk or dawn, when the light is poor, the distinctive white rump patch of the hawk, or the blunt head of the owl, can be difficult to detect. When in doubt, watch for a fast or slow wing beat. To a person familiar with either bird the sight of the other will show a notable difference.

As we approached the area a pair of Red-winged Blackbirds rose from the ground and pursued the flying owl each time its circles approached their home. These aerial battles were revealing examples of the deceptiveness of speed in relation to size. Here at an angle above us we could see that the owl was stalling, possibly waiting for the humans to approach closer, but in spite of his sluggish attitude the Red-wings had

Short-eared in flight, about to attack

to extend power to their utmost to attain and maintain a position above him. When the angle was right—with the owl below and in front—one of the smaller birds with a final burst would hurtle toward him. But to the owl this was a familiar tactic. Without breaking his glide or quickening a wing beat, he waited until only ten or twelve inches of space separated him from the attacking bird and then, seemingly without visible effort, would pivot on his back with talons upraised to meet the charge. Another deceptive action consisted of a powerful push with half-closed wings just before contact was made. When this was done the Red-wing would be left fighting thin air, with the owl regaining normal flight along a horizontal stretch a score of feet below.

Although we couldn't tell the exact position of the nest, when a second owl joined the flight its location was almost pinpointed. However, I was due for a surprise. As we proceeded, one of the pair dropped from a height of fifty feet and delayed veering away from our heads until only three feet away. This happened many times, and I found myself ducking the menacing closeness of the bird's approach. As we shifted position, the owl also changed the direction of its dives. If we walked in a circle the direction of her dive compensated for any point of the compass. At the center of our imaginary circle, a half-grown young one was found stretched flat on the ground, completely immobile. Although the owlet was only three weeks old and covered with the soft down of infancy, he was at least fifty feet from the nest. Four others were found scattered throughout the grasses, all distantly separated one from the other. There was some evidence that they reconvened at meal times or possibly at a command from one of the parents.

Bits of driftwood and other flotsam showed that on occasion the nesting area was subject to floods when extreme winds pushed high tide crests farther than usual. According to Urner, this had happened in the past and he was of the opinion that the adults possibly moved either eggs or small young from danger. However, he was reluctant to make a definite statement to this effect, probably remembering the unproved legendary stories that credit Whip-poor-wills and others of the nighthawk group with the same trait.

Urner sometimes witnessed the wounded bird ruse. According to him, such antics usually started after a dive or two failed to drive away an intruder. The disturbed bird would then fly in the air and maintain a position facing into the wind. If the day was calm the position would be maintained by hovering, but if windy, the bird was held aloft on rigid open wings. The pause seemed to be designed to give the bird time to deliberate, or possibly just to be noticed before dropping to the ground. The descents took two forms: the more common of these was accomplished by plummeting with half-closed wings, but the rarer descent was the more spectacular. In this the bird actually tumbled through the air as though stopped in flight by a charge of shot. On reaching the ground—which, from Urner's version, was done feet first with wings outspread—the bird would carefully fold one wing to its side and draw attention with the other by waving it flag-like in the air.

Sometimes the wounded-bird act was totally silent, but some pairs that Urner had encountered in the Jersey swamps habitually squealed during the action as though in great distress. Others would groan and make a pretense of hiding in a dense bush or weed pile, beating the bushes with their wings as though to make sure they would be detected and followed.

Some of the preliminary flight phases of this wounded-bird act are similar to parts of their air-borne courtship. Luring of an enemy away from a nest usually starts from an overhead position and the ground is reached in a zooming dive or by tumbling. Similar descents are used, presumably by the male, to impress the female, but in the day or night courtship flights, sounds conveying romantic intentions accompany these acrobatics, and are produced not only by vocal means but also by vibrating wings. If the hypothesis that owls are distant evolutionary relatives of goatsuckers, nighthawks, Whip-poor-wills, and so forth is correct, it dates back through many geological ages, for the present-day nighthawk courtship is similar.

Throughout the evolution of owls, one of the main developments reached its peak in the silent flight. Yet with the Short-eared, there is a deliberate attempt to negate this valuable asset when, during spring and summer, they produce a brisk flapping noise by bringing their primaries together; it sounds like a flag snapping in a high wind and can be heard for long distances. Although this action is generally regarded as pertaining to courtship, some observers have noticed it several months after the nesting season. Noise from wings is not unknown in the bird world. Hummingbirds and nighthawks produce it by vibrating feathers at the termination of dives, and some of the doves produce sound by clapping their wings together while in flight. Just offhand, however, I believe that the Short-eared Owls are the only species to use a combination of the two methods, clapping of wings and positioning of feathers, to obtain audible wind vibration.

Short-eared Owls seem to be present throughout the year in most areas where they nest in temperate zones. However, it is possible that there is shifting of populations, with birds of the far north taking the place of some more southern breeders that in turn have moved farther south. The effect of permanency would thus be maintained even though gained by a shifting population. At the edge of the arctic circle the Short-ears are a more common bird than the traditional Snowy, but those in the far north do not wait for food shortages to force them southward as do their large white cousins. Instead they seemingly move in large flocks. This southern journey is somewhat nomadic, without a preconceived destination. However, some sixth sense seems to lead many of the travelers to areas where mice are especially abundant. When such spots are found, the owls stay until the rodent population is brought back to normal. If ornithological history were to be thoroughly perused there would be very few areas within the tremendous range of these owls that have not at some time in the past been benefitted by their invasions.

In my pursuit of owls I have been fortunate enough to see two of their winter invasions, both in California—one in Imperial Valley and one in the San Joaquin. In both instances, well over fifty birds were present and while some perched on fence posts or other prominent spots, a like number circled the fields using a technique of hunting similar to that of Marsh Hawks. Charles W. Townsend, in A. C. Bent's *Life Histories of North American Birds of Prey*, says of these congregations:

"When field mice or voles increase so as to become veritable plagues, various owls, especially of this species [Short-eared], have been known to congregate in the infested region and to have done great service in destroying the pests. There are several such records in various counties in England extending back to the sixteenth century. Such a plague of mice is described by Hudson (1892) as occurring in South America in 1872–73, when short-eared owls were most important agents in stopping the plague."

Despite their value, proved through the centuries in many parts of the world, Short-eared Owls are consistently shot by thoughtless gunners. However, better days may be forecast for the owls in the future, for when Bakersfield, California, had its rodent plague, in the winter of 1926/27 with an estimated four hundred to four thousand mice per acre, the United States Biological Survey sent an expert on rodent control and his first move was to protect rigidly all the hawks and owls in the region. His diagnosis was that earlier killing of these birds and other predators had permitted a population explosion of rodents, their normal foods. If such evidence makes its way into popular media, perhaps the wanton killing of these birds will stop.

MEASUREMENTS   Length 13–17 inches; wingspread 42 inches.

VOICE   Many owls are so nocturnal that their actions when uttering calls are largely the result of an observer's guesswork, but since Short-eared have a twenty-four-hour working day, the calls can be seen as well as heard. One of the strangest of their calls is one in courtship, consisting of a rapidly repeated series of low hoots with no variation in pitch. Although hoots are to be expected from owls, these utterances differ from most by having a ventriloquistic quality that makes the calling bird very difficult to locate. Alexander DuBois describes it as " 'Toot-toot-toot-toot-toot'-etc. . . . repeated fifteen to twenty times, at the rate of four toots per second, in a low-pitched monotone," which seemed to come from all directions. Whenever he observed the calling bird it was flying high in the air on wings that were rapidly beating to maintain altitude but not much forward speed.

On one occasion at my short-lived Colorado nest, a bird barely discernible in the grasses behind the eggs uttered a squealing, groaning cry as though in agony. A bird given to the Arizona-Sonora Desert Museum with a slightly injured wing uttered a call during treatment similar to the screech of a Barn Owl. The only noticeable difference between this call and that of the Barn Owl was its intensity: the voice of the Short-eared did not threaten to ruin eardrums.

NESTING   A nest of Short-eared Owls found off the ground is exceptional. On very rare occasions, usually in salt areas where tides must be contended with, they have been found in low bushes, but even then they are placed so low as to have some of the nest material dragging on the ground.

The usual site is a scooped-out depression, which is then lined with dry grasses, reeds, and some feathers, until a platform about two inches off the ground is achieved. Most, if not all, of this nesting material consists of growth immediately available within

Nesting Short-eared on the Colorado plains,
just before a hailstorm shattered its eggs

a few yards of the nest, and much of it is pulled or nipped from its roots while green. A few nests have been found where normal growth has been allowed to stand and forms a dome over the incubating bird, but on many there is no attempt at nest concealment.

John and Frank Craighead feel that Short-eared Owls prefer to nest in grasses that blend with their plumage, and during their research on predatory birds in Michigan finally learned to by-pass dark-colored areas; ". . . and with this clue in mind, all fields of tall light-colored grass as well as grass sedge kettles and marsh areas were searched."

Although it has long been known that Short-eared Owls have a tendency to colonize and return to the same breeding area year after year, Charles Urner was the first to find that they sometimes actually rebuild old nests. In the same marsh I visited with him many years ago he found a newly constructed nest with eggs. Beneath the new set, however, there was an old discolored egg of the year before. The top section of the nesting material showed that a new platform had been built upon an old one much weathered by winter storms.

As with any wide-ranging species of bird, it would be hard to find one whose habits weren't altered by local conditions. This has occurred on the island of Oomlashka, where William H. Dall, after whom the Dall sheep (*Ovis dalli*) of Alaska was named, found Short-eared Owls breeding in burrows. As he described the nesting, " . . . the hole is horizontal, and the inner end usually a little higher than the aperture; lined with dry grass and feathers." The burrows were not over two feet deep, usually excavated in the side of a steep bank.

Charles W. Townsend says of the eggs: "The short-eared owl may lay anywhere from four to nine eggs, and rarely even more; but the commonest numbers are five, six, or seven. The eggs vary in shape from oval to elliptical-ovate. The shell is smooth, or very finely granulated, with very little, if any, gloss. The color is white, or very faintly creamy white." The measurements of fifty-six eggs in the United States National Museum average 39 × 31 mm.

HOURS OF ACTIVITY   If there is any definite time when Short-eared Owls sleep it is known only to them. Spend a day distantly watching a nesting colony, and you will usually notice that some birds are always on the move. Toward dusk

activity accelerates a little but not enough to call the birds crepuscular; and then with darkness, when hearing is forced to take the place of sight, come the calls, sometimes from close overhead, sometimes from a distance. Activity counts made by sight, or counts made by sound, are difficult to correlate. In the latter, is it one loquacious bird or several that are carrying on conversations? Frankly, I don't know, and many other observers prefer to evade the same question.

In spite of the fact that most observers feel that Short-eared Owls are equally adept by day or by night, some of their diurnal activities might result from the abundance or scarcity of prey, with more work hours necessary if the latter condition prevails. The Craigheads explain the situation as witnessed in Michigan: "The owls generally left the roost about dusk, several rising at a time and quartering the fields near by before disappearing in the distance. They were never observed hunting during the day, and it was difficult to flush them before 4 p.m. The Short-eared Owl is noted for its diurnal hunting, being especially active in daylight hours during the nesting season, but those observed during the winter of 1941–42 remained on the roost throughout the day. It is probable that the abundance of meadow mice permitted the owls to obtain sufficient food between dusk and dawn, and hence there was no need for daylight hunting. The large number of hawks with which they would have had to compete may also have discouraged diurnal hunting."

FOOD   Most investigators would rightfully claim that mice are the staple diet of these owls. A. K. Fisher reports that of 101 stomachs examined, 11 contained small birds; 77, mice; 7, other mammals; 7, insects; and 14 were empty. In 137 pellets of these birds examined, the identifiable remains of 110 small mammals and 3 birds were found. Paul Errington, in *The Condor*, July 1932, mentions the Wisconsin foods as determined from pellets as: meadow mice, 68; deer mice, 115; Snow Bunting, 1; Meadowlark, 1. Almost all available food records for the species are similar, but where exceptions have been found they are truly astounding. William Brewster's old record at Muskeget Island, Massachusetts, is one of the exceptions. A small colony of Short-eared Owls nested in close proximity to a large colony of terns and seemingly the owls were content to feed entirely on this feathered prey. Over fifty tern carcasses were found that had had nothing but breasts and entrails eaten. J. A. Munro reports on another exception seen on a marsh near Toronto, Canada, in an area of about fifty

13

SAW-WHET OWLS

In the years immediately following my Flushing, Long Island, experience with Barn Owls—the study that made me a devotee of owls—I became employed as a nature counselor at several boys' camps. One of the camps was in Maine and two in upper New York State. According to DeWitt Miller, Frank Chapman, and Edward Forbush, all these spots were ideal for the finding of nesting Saw-whet Owls. These eminent naturalists were sympathetic with my owl-seeking, and to help in my search, told me to tap on the base of any tree containing a Flicker hole that was from ten to thirty feet from the ground. Nesting Saw-whets might answer my knock.

So for the next three summer seasons I tapped tall trees, short trees, stumps, or in fact anything that contained the slightest resemblance to a cavity. Before many days had passed, I even had the campers tapping and though some of them didn't know what to look for, they would dutifully lay down their axes, their canteens, knapsacks, first aid kits, and other paraphernalia that encumbered hiking and rap on the trunk of a tree. If owls had cooperated as did my young charges, this chapter could be based on personal observations instead of mainly on the field notes of others.

Saw-whets, however, failed to react to the knock, maintaining strict secrecy. When I was about to conclude that the birds didn't exist in the terrain which we worked,

Saw-whet Owl

three young in juvenile plumage were encountered on a branch. These birds, which must have emerged from a nearby nest, had little resemblance to the adults of the species. Their over-all color was a rich, dark mahogany brown with no trace of the breast streaking prominent on older birds. Above the beak and stretching from eye to eye was a triangle of white, which set off even more the over-all rich brown.

Although these youngsters, when first approached, spread their wings and snapped their beaks in a futile attempt to appear ferocious, they permitted themselves to be picked up and we examined their beautiful first-year plumage. As a rule most parent owls will show themselves when their young are disturbed, but these, of Waterton, Maine, remained out of sight. A diligent search was made for the nest but we didn't find it. An hour later the young had disappeared, possibly lured away by parents, whom we could hear in dense growth uttering robin-like whistles.

If such a ruse was used, this pair of birds was showing their nesting season secretiveness, which is almost entirely lacking in those Saw-whet Owls that wander southward in winter. Aside from the Spotted Owls, Saw-whets are usually considered to be the most trusting of the group, especially when forced by deep snows to forsake their nesting territory. I remember a nature walk in New York's Central Park many years ago led by Ludlow Griscom of the American Museum. In a small shrub the party discovered an adult Saw-whet that was handled by at least half a dozen people and then replaced on its chosen perch. After such treatment most birds would have moved to a new location, but this one returned to the same branch for many days and did not seem overly disturbed by recurrent examinations.

It is not likely that set rules will ever apply to the southward movements of most owls. The various species cannot be lumped together like quail and called sedentary. Nor can they be likened to Flycatchers, southern migrations being almost a certainty. Some owls, such as Screech and Horned, are almost permanent residents, usually spending their entire lives in a limited area. A few species, and this definitely applies to Snowy Owls, make limited movements in the far north but not extensively into the United States unless food shortages force them southward. Short-eared Owls seemingly shift from place to place in large bands and often winter in areas where mouse plagues are occurring. Elf Owls disappear from Arizona when insects become scarce and suddenly reappear in numbers in the spring.

Whether these movements are accomplished in large flocks or singly, by long

flights or short hops, is really not known about most owls, but there is a slight clue in regard to Saw-whets. On several occasions when I lived in the east I saw Saw-whets appear where they definitely had not been the day before; once three turned up in a small woodland area of less than an acre.

That the most northern nesters of the species sometimes move in massed flight is partially proven by an October occurrence on Lake Huron following a severe storm. Almost two thousand birds of mixed species were picked up along two miles of shore-line and about two dozen of these storm-killed birds were Saw-whet Owls. On another occasion, also on Lake Huron and also during October, the captain of a steamer witnessed a large migration of small owls. Whether this was a nocturnal or diurnal flight is not mentioned. Many of them alighted on the steamer rigging. Little if anything is known about their northward journeys, but by March most that have wintered in the south will have disappeared from their non-nesting winter range to rejoin those that survived the rigors of the north.

In spite of a trusting nature, which verges on the foolish, combined with a range that covers much of the northern United States and parts of Canada, Saw-whet Owl nests are still comparatively rare. Possibly the trust they exhibit in the winter months changes in the breeding season; if this is so, there is a possibility that many of the cavity trees I tapped on for three seasons had owls within that did not show themselves. But I would hate to be forced to test this supposition by carrying a ladder over those interminable miles.

A. C. Bent's *Life Histories of North American Birds of Prey* lists numerous instances of Saw-whets responding to a tap on a nesting tree by perching at the cavity entrance. Some of the birds disturbed while incubating would fly out and perch on a branch six or eight feet away and calmly wait while a climber examined the nesting hole. One account mentions a bird that barely waited for a human hand to be removed before it flew to the nest and dropped down inside the hollow. However, in any animal species there are individualists—some wild, some tame. With Saw-whets in the breeding season I haven't been able to locate either temperament.

Most published reports intimate that nesting territories in forested areas either have water nearby or are, in themselves, slightly swampy. Saw-whets usually prefer holes excavated by Flickers, but they have been known to nest in natural cavities and there are one or two old records of them nesting in the open nests of other birds. As

the ground on boughs, their bodies snug against the main trunk of the tree, but as nesters they have been found at least seventy-five feet from the earth. It is generally conceded that they do not embellish a cavity with any nesting material but instead use it as found.

Bent states in regard to eggs: "The saw-whet owl lays four to seven eggs, five or six being the commonest numbers. The eggs are usually oval in shape, but sometimes slightly ovate or more nearly globular. The shell is smooth, with little or no gloss, and the color is pure white." The average of fifty-two eggs is 29.9×25 mm.

HOURS OF ACTIVITY
Although the Saw-whets are generally considered to be strictly nocturnal, some of the prey they use as food is definitely diurnal. The diurnal items that have been reported on their menu (all definitely atypical of their normal diet) are chipmunks, young red squirrels, sparrows, juncos, and warblers. These are creatures that shun the darkness, but it might be that in the subdued light of the woodland where Saw-whets generally reside, some daylight hunting is carried on out of sight of human observers. One wintering bird I discovered in the late afternoon on Long Island held a deer mouse in its talons. When he was scared into dropping it, it was found that the stiffening of rigor mortis had not set in, which, although circumstantial, makes me believe that, when given the prey and the desire, daylight hunting sometimes occurs.

FOOD
The food of the Saw-whets is predictable for owls of their size. Mice of all kinds, with deer or white-footed preferred, probably make up the majority of the items on their food list. In addition they will take the young of red squirrels and rats. Chipmunks, shrews, and bats have also been recorded as food, as have sparrows, juncos, and warblers. A. K. Fisher reports on 22 stomachs examined: 17 contained mice; 1, a bird; 1, an insect; and 3 were empty. There is one record of an individual killing pigeons, seven in one night—a valiant little bird, since even the smallest of pigeon breeds outweighs Saw-whets two to one or more.

Following a knock on the tree
where it was nesting, a Saw-whet peers out

14

A POTPOURRI OF FACTS

Naturalists have written millions of words in their research on birds, but unfortunately the remarkable information they have gleaned is widely scattered. Works have appeared in a score of languages and in various formats—from strictly ornithological publications to obscure notes of small institutions. Therefore, although almost all facets of the lives of a great many birds have been subjected to study, the job of "researching the research" often entails more time and labor than the original investigation. And no matter how diligent the quest, something of interest almost always escapes the researcher.

There are some writers who have a flair for the popular along with their scientific expertise, and, in fact, it is the popularization of science that is in large measure responsible for increasing our knowledge of bird life. In the generalized chapter that follows I have drawn heavily on the work of three such popularizers, with their permission—Roger Tory Peterson, Peter Farb, and the late Arthur Allen.

PRIMITIVE BEGINNINGS The conditions permitting the fossilization of birds are much more critical than those attending the fossilization of solid-boned mammals and reptiles, and, as a result, the family tree of owl evolution is fragmentary. However, enough fossil forms have been uncovered to make us believe that the first true owls appeared during the Eocene, or a little over fifty million years ago. These were round-headed owls named generically *Protostrix* and placed in a family called the Protostrigidae. The Oligocene apparently evolved the first of the eared, or horned, groups, the probable ancestors of the Long-eared and Horned Owls (family Strigidae) of the present day. Their origin dates back about thirty-six million years. Ten million years later, during the Miocene, ancestors of the Barn Owl (family Tytonidae) appeared. In that same age owls of the genus *Strix* had evolved, somewhat similar to our present-day Barred and Spotted Owls. Nothing outstanding has yet been uncovered about these nocturnal birds during the twelve-million-year period covering the Pliocene, although evolutionary changes were no doubt occurring just as they are today.

It was during the Pleistocene that seemingly the greatest development in owls took place, and the word "seemingly" is being used purposely with respect to this relatively recent age, stretching from nearly two million years ago to a mere 11,000 years ago. Traces of these creatures of bygone ages are bound to be preserved better if laid down as fossils during the last million years, rather than 50 million years earlier. So the Pleistocene (seemingly) evolved many comparatively small owls, such as the Burrowing, Screech, and Pygmy. John Hamlet and Shelly and Mary Louise Grossman in their masterful book *Birds of Prey of the World* have brought out the fact that seed-bearing plants began to appear in the Miocene, and with this new and ubiquitous food, small rodents began to proliferate in great numbers. During millions of years, nature recognized the need to control and challenge the ascendancy of these creatures by evolving small predators proportionate to size of the prey—proportions that most of them maintain to this day.

Just a glance at these changes shows that the owls, for one, have now developed a very efficient pattern suitable to their existence in the world they now live in. But if they had existed in those ages when ponderous dinosaurs, giant ground sloths, saber-toothed tigers, and huge pachyderms roamed the earth, they would have been as incongruous as such enormously massive creatures would be now.

CLOSEST RELATIVES OF OWLS   Not long ago hawks and owls were considered closely related, with the first hunting primarily by day and the latter hunting mainly at night. They were all lumped together (and still are) under

the term "birds of prey," and early books on ornithology always listed them in the same or adjoining chapters. It was a convenient system based on the similarity of their foods, their habits and beneficial qualities; but in terms of evolution and anatomy, it was false. Present-day ornithologists separate the hawks and the owls with many other bird families, usually placing the owls near the nightjars and goatsuckers (Nighthawks, Whip-poor-wills).

EYESIGHT
"Myth information" about owls is widespread and the old saying "blind as an owl" is deeply implanted in the minds of laymen. In reality owls have superb eyesight, and although they are specialized for night vision, they can see very well in daylight. So efficient is their vision that at least one species of owl can capture prey where the light is only equivalent to that thrown by an ordinary candle burning twenty-five hundred feet away.

This incredible efficiency is the result of many factors, one of the most important being eye size. Compared to the optical equipment of humans in relation to body bulk, owl eyes are many times greater. And, like some expensive lenses, the iris of their eyes has such a versatile diaphragm that it can "stop down" to a mere pinpoint in the bright glare of intense sunlight or "open wide" to pick up the reflected light of a dim illumination hundreds of yards away. This ability is not confined to the use of both eyes at once, but is capable of being exercised by either eye completely independent of the other.

But despite astounding vision in almost every degree of light owls have one disadvantage, for their eyeballs are fixed—like headlights on a car. Therefore, to see in different directions they are endowed with an extraordinary ability to rotate heads—not, as in myths, all the way around to ring their necks, but revolving for three quarters of a turn, possibly more, before whipping back to start rotating from the starting point again. The action is so rapid that it appears to be one fluid motion. Whereas the eyes of most birds are placed on the sides of the head, the eyes of owls are placed directly in front on a comparatively wide skull—and thus they provide completely binocular vision. But most owls, as though not satisfied with binocular vision for the judging of distance, will often go through a series of bobs and swaying motions that increase their eyes' effectiveness by triangulation.

Just how effective can an eye be? It seems that with a preponderance of light-gathering rod cells in the eye an owl's sight is almost beyond improvement, already

As demonstrated by this Great Horned Owl,
owls can dilate their pupils independently of one another

Not yet registering the brilliance of the photographic flash,
an Elf Owl's pupils dilate widely to see in virtual darkness

adapted to make full use of every glint of available light. However, owls also have "visual purple," a chemical aid to sight, which will be discussed in the following section.

COLOR BLINDNESS   The optical apparatus of humans and many other animals focuses a scene on both rod and cone cells. The latter transmit all the shades of the spectrum to the brain and give complete color vision. However, color as such depends on light, and when that fades the most brilliant shades lose their vividness and become variations from black to white. The rod cells also have light-gathering propensities and without our normal quota of them we would be confronted with walls of black as soon as nightfall settled. Claustrophobia might be a common reaction to such intense blackness.

In the evolution of owls the ability to gather light appears to have been of far greater importance than any values derived from detecting color. Consequently cones did not hold a dominant place in owl evolutionary development. The rods, however, were a necessity and became tightly packed for night vision. Such vision makes the owls of today live in a world colored only by various shades of gray.

The light-gathering rods that owls possess in such abundance have a further aid — a remarkable chemical known as "visual purple." This fluid converts even the slightest glimmer of light into a chemical signal that is flashed to the brain, giving these nocturnal birds an actual image impression. Under similar circumstances a human being would see only the presence of light.

However, there are evidently other factors about which we know little or nothing that also aid an owl's night sight, for Dr. Casey Albert Wood in his book *The Fundus Oculi of Birds* has found that all the *Strigiformes* (owls) ophthalmoscopically examined by him have "a preponderance of yellow in their eyegrounds. Without carrying this assertion too far we note that in semi-nocturnal Owls . . . the red tints overpower the yellow and a shade of orange results." He carries this even further into other species of birds and postulates that "an admixture of yellow (in the form of an orange-red coloration) may be present to indicate not so much recent as former, i.e., atavistic, night habits long since abandoned." He feels that "There are so few exceptions to the rule of the yellow-colored fundus in Night Birds that one may confidently assert that the amount of this color in avian (one might say in all vertebrate) fundi is in direct ratio to the proportionate use a given species makes of its visual powers after sunset."

EYE SHINE Many nocturnal animals, and some diurnal, have eye shine that varies greatly not only in degree and intensity, but also in color. The illegal hunting of deer at night called 'jack-lighting" is performed by directing the beam of a flashlight across an area where deer are known to occur. If one of the animals looks toward the light, and if the flash is held near the eye of the hunter, the two glowing orbs of the prey will be reflected back with unbelievable intensity.

Colors of eye shine reflection differ according to the species of animal being "jack-lighted." Deer eyes are usually silvery-white, coyotes greenish-white, kit fox reddish. Each class of animals seems to have some members capable of creating such inner reflection. This trait is very apparent in some fish, and the multiple eyes of the desert wolf spider glow like tiny diamonds when a beam of light strikes them. The eyes of birds in the family known as goatsuckers, which contains the Poor-wills and Nighthawks, glow like tiny red electric bulbs in a beam of light.

Considering the relative evolutionary closeness of owls and goatsuckers, and the extreme eye shine of some, if not all, of the latter, I thought there might be some differentiation between owls that were largely diurnal (Short-eared, Hawk Owl, Burrowing, and Snowy) and those largely nocturnal (Barn, Long-eared, Elf, and Screech). Eye shine, according to Stewart Duke-Elder in *System of Ophthalmology*, volume 1, ". . . aids vision in dim illumination." A part of a pertinent paragraph is quoted as follows: "A tapetum lucidum is an accessory to the optical system to aid vision in dim illumination; it is essentially a mirror-arrangement so that light, having traversed the sentient elements of the retina, is reflected backwards again and its effective intensity is thus augmented. Not only is the amount of light available for stimulation thus materially increased but slight differences in luminosity between an object and its background are proportionately accentuated so that the total effectivity of vision in dim illumination is correspondingly improved. It is this reflected light seen by an observer standing beyond the animal's near-point . . . which gives rise to the striking 'eye-shine.'" A footnote states: "The effective intensity would theoretically be doubled by a perfect mirror. A tapetum probably insures an increase of about half as much—forty per cent in the cat."

With such information proving that eye shine is a tremendous aid to night vision, and the close relationship between the eye-shining goatsuckers and owls, researchers attempted, through flashlight tests on a number of captive owls, to assess relative eye-shine strengths:

RELATIVE EYE-SHINE STRENGTHS

SPECIES	EYE-SHINE COLOR	RELATIVE BRILLIANCE
Yellow Iris		
Screech Owl	red	weak
Burrowing Owl	none	
Long-eared Owl	slightly red	strong
Great Horned Owl	red	medium
Elf Owl	none	
Short-eared Owl	red	weak
Brown Iris		
Spotted Owl	red	strong
Barred Owl	red	strong
Barn Owl	red	weak

From these cursory views, based mainly on captive specimens, no real pattern for the family as a whole is evident, such as stronger shine on those that hunt almost entirely by night and a weaker shine on those primarily diurnal, even though the observations on diurnal Burrowing Owls might seem to substantiate such a condition.

Yellow-irised owls and solid-brown-eyed owls do not even fit into a reasonable pattern, for the Barn, the Barred, and Spotted belong to the latter group, and the shine is barely detectable in Barn Owls but is strong in Barred and Spotted. Those examined with yellow irises are the Elf, the Horned, the Long-eared, the Screech, and Burrowing. All but the Burrowing showed shine in varying degrees. Since the Burrowing Owl is the only species examined that could be considered primarily diurnal, it would seem that greater amounts of natural light during a bird's most active period would reduce the amount of shine needed. However, until more diurnal owls—such as Short-eared, Hawk Owls, Snowy Owls, and Pygmy Owls—are tested, any conclusion would be premature. These primary tests were made with an eight-volt unfiltered flashlight beam.

The Elf Owl is a species with yellow-irised eyes

*All owls have cloudy pupils when they are young. The phenomenon
is particularly noticeable on these growing Spotted Owls*

In color-corrected strobe and flashlight photos taken at the wildlife blind at the Arizona-Sonora Desert Museum the images registered on color film show intense eye shine on both Screech and Horned Owls. So it may be that light, correctly filtered and under scientifically controlled conditions, might give an entirely different picture to eye shine in owls, such as distinguishing the nocturnal from the diurnal, or even evolutionary relationships. It seems to me that this is an interesting problem for some young investigator to pursue with proper controls and precision instruments not available to me.

EYELIDS AND NICTITATING MEMBRANES

Most birds, to cleanse an eye of dust or foreign particles, raise the lower eyelid, but owls drop the upper eyelid instead when blinking. High-speed photos also show that the upper lid is closed momentarily when an owl comes in contact with living prey. The nictitating membrane, a transparent covering that slides from the inner corner outward, is present in all birds, as well as many reptiles and mammals, but operates so rapidly that it is difficult to detect in motion. Owls, however, especially young ones, sometimes pass it over the entire eye in a slow-motion manner that is plainly visible. As a highly functional part of the complicated eyes of owls, the nictitating membrane's main purpose is to carry moisture from lid to lid.

CLOUDY PUPILS OF YOUNG
Changes of eye color, indicative of immaturity or adulthood, and winter or breeding season, are not unusual among birds. The young of all owls start with gray or milky pupils that, soon after flying age, change to dark brown or almost black. This early milky appearance is very noticeable on the brown-eyed owls such as Barred and Barn, but not so apparent on those with pupils surrounded by a yellow iris. There also seems to be a slight change in the color of the iris of yellow-irised owls during the breeding season. On some it is yellow throughout most of the year but it attains an orange tint just prior to and during the nesting season.

HEARING
To excel in one specialty, such as eyesight, would seem enough for any one avian family, but owls do not stop here. Their hearing is equally wondrous, so efficient that by hearing alone, some—and perhaps all—of them can use it

instead of sight on the darkest nights. Half a century ago, when I made my protracted study of Barn Owls, there were factors influencing the capture of prey that puzzled me. Any prolonged dry spell would cause a nightly increase in the rodent food brought to the nest of young; a touch of humidity, however, would cause the capture graph to slide downward, and rain would subject the young to a starvation diet. I racked my brain for explanations and arrived at certain conclusions that at the time had to remain mere supposition in the absence of proof (see Chapter 1 for a fuller discussion of these).

The possibility I gave least consideration to was the audibility of a rodent moving on wet as opposed to dry ground, on wet instead of dry leaves. The difference in sound produced would be so negligible, it seemed to me, that it could be completely discounted. Therefore the quandary remained. A few years ago, however, Roger Payne, then a graduate student at Cornell University, became interested in unraveling the puzzle, substituting unproved theory and guesswork with actual fact.

In his experiments Payne carefully sealed all the openings in a long shed so that the building was completely light-tight. Then dry leaves were spread on the floor and a Barn Owl given its freedom within until it had become accustomed to its dark surroundings. Time after time live mice were released and for just a moment Payne could hear the liberated rodent move in the dry leaves. Then he felt a draft of air as the owl left its perch and dived to the floor. When the light was snapped on, Payne found the owl with mouse in talons. He tried the experiment time after time with almost unvarying results.

Owls were changed to make sure that the ability existed for the species, and was not just the ability of a single individual. Those from the far west, those from the east, and some I sent him from Arizona all performed in a similar manner. Final confirmation that the owls executed their feats solely through the use of their acute hearing came when Payne commenced plugging the owls' ears. When this was done the owls went wide of their mark, baffled because they were deprived of the triangulation that sound gave to their aim. Unplugging the ears of one that had missed brought accuracy again as well as the demise of another mouse.

Much of an owl's amazing hearing is due to the remarkable structure of its ears. The ear openings of some species are so large that they almost cover the wide sides of the head, and the fact that the ears are set far apart enhances the triangulation of

tainted meat that a human being would detect when several feet away can be tossed to a semi-tame owl and it will be attacked immediately. After the first bite, however, it will be pushed aside and not eaten. Such actions point toward taste and not olfactory perception even though the two are closely related. However, contradicting the above are the numerous reports by trappers that recount the trapping of Horned Owls baited solely by scent and not with a visible bait such as a carcass or piece of meat.

To further confuse the issue are the attacks by Horned Owls on skunks. Where these mammals abound it is exceptional to find a Horned Owl that does not carry taints of such encounters. Some of these could be the result of a false identification of a mammal on the ground, but if this is true the memory of owls is poor indeed. Furthermore, on my visits to several score of Horned Owl homes I have found a striped skunk in one nest, and traces in four others, showing that even if capture were a matter of mistaken identity the owls still utilized the catch as food. That they are eaten by owls is extraordinary, for road-kills of skunks, judging by the length of time their remains stay on highways, are not—like rabbits or squirrels—preferred food of other predators.

All five of my owl nests contained only striped skunks, despite the fact that the smaller spotted skunk also abounded in the area. Although I realize that judgment should not be based on merely five observations, there is the possibility that the owls could catch the larger striped variety without receiving a full, nauseating blast from the skunk's musk atomizer. The smaller spotted skunk, however, is the only one of four species found in the United States that habitually aims the scent vertically upward—a feat accomplished by standing on the two front legs, with the hind legs and rear raised high in the air. Further observations may show that this anti-aircraft device, which can hit an owl when it is still a yard or more away, renders these small skunks immune to owl attacks.

NOISELESS FEATHERS   Besides owls' modified ears and eyes, there are still other anatomical features that set them apart from all other birds. Their feathers, aside from those of the stiff-rimmed facial disk, are constructed in such a way as to make their flight almost noiseless. The flight feathers have downy edges that eliminate most of the whirr caused by the stiff primaries of other birds as they cut the air.

Peter Farb aptly describes their softness when he quotes Alexander Wilson: ". . .

A sure way of distinguishing the common Screech Owl
from the rare Spotted is the difference
between their lead primary feathers. Here, Spotted is at top, Screech Owl below

may be touched without being felt." The softness of the feathers seems less pronounced on the owls that are largely diurnal or that feed primarily on insects or arachnids. Elf, Burrowing, Pygmy, and Hawk Owls all make an audible swishing noise when they fly.

THE "EAR" TUFTS

The feather tufts on the heads of some species are often miscalled "ears." They are more than merely ornamental, for they are an integral part of their owners' protective form. Undisturbed, most of the tufted owls allow these plumes to relax and lie against the back of the head. At the slightest sign of danger, however, they lift them to a vertical position, partially shut the eyes, and align the facial feathers into vertical lines (see the five-second sequence on Screech Owls). If, as in the case of the Screech Owl, the background used is rough bark, the resultant blend is very effective: when an owl is perched on a stump, the two jagged feather tufts become the splinters of a broken bough that can either camouflage the bird from its enemies or perhaps permit the closer approach of desired prey.

THE TALONS

As an owl approaches prey with intent to kill, the talons at the outset of the flight are drawn close to the body like fists, but when the remaining distance is right, a downward swoop on noiseless wings will bring them into the open position on straightened legs. And what four-pronged mousetraps these talons are! Each leg has a thick tendon that runs down and around what on our foot would be the heel, creating a peculiar sort of sliding pulley. This tendon branches to the four needle-sharp talons, which are widespread at the termination of the dive. In fact, when their legs are straight out, owls lose the ability to tighten their grip. At the moment of impact, however, the legs draw up, as much because of momentum and the sudden stop as because of the owl's desire to cart away the prize. The tendon in the "pulley-leg" draws on the toes and the talons are driven home. As long as the legs remain bent, the talons stay imbedded. On several occasions I have been grabbed by an angry owl, and if the owl's legs were permitted to remain bent and close to the bird's body, even prying would not release the pressure. If the legs were forcibly straightened, however, as they would be in a foot-first dive, the tendon-lock would be weakened and extrication would become possible. My owl studies became less painful when I learned this fact!

Sequence photographs show how a Screech Owl
uses its ear tufts as a camouflage device

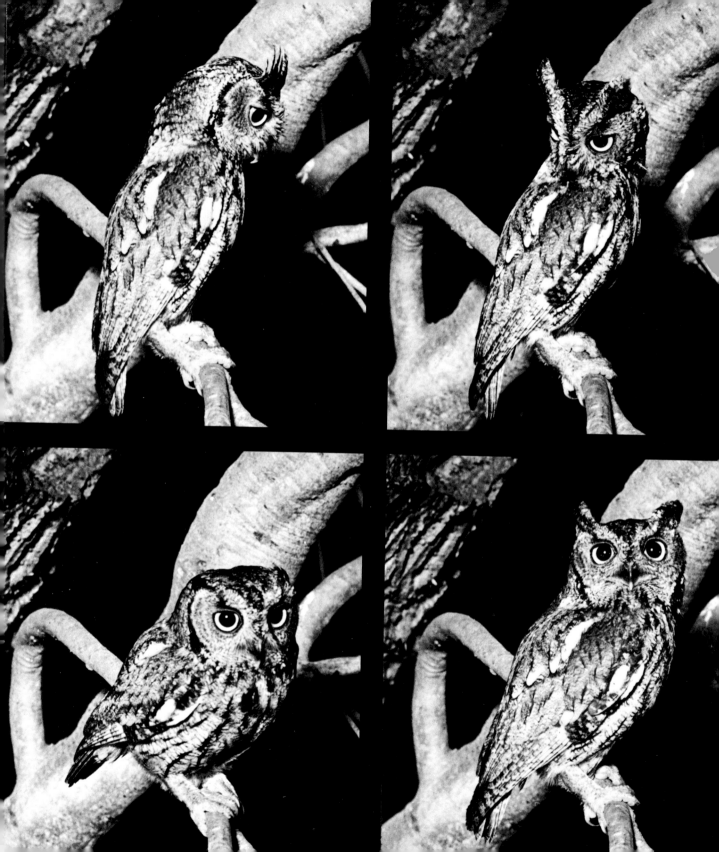

Two Saw-whet Owls illustrate the size difference between sexes — the male is the smaller

SEX DIFFERENCES   In many of the higher forms of wildlife the male of the species is the larger and presumably the stronger, or—if sizes are equal—the male is better equipped with horns, tusks, talons, or what-have-you to fight for survival. With predatory birds, however, there is a reversal, which I believe runs throughout all the hawks and owls to a greater or lesser degree. It is so pronounced in some of the larger falcons that the term "tiercel" (which means roughly "one-third smaller") was applied to the male Peregrine in the old days of falconry and remains in use today.

Although this sex difference is not as obvious in owls, it is there nevertheless and may even be detected in the field if a pair is situated where a comparison can be made. By all the rules of the game this size difference should give a higher voice to the small males and a lower one to the females. Alden Miller, referring to his earlier study on the vocal apparatus of owls in *The Condor* (September 1934), stated in 1947: "It was shown that the cross-section of the air passages corresponds in general with body size. The larger the species the larger is the syringeal segment of the air passages and the longer the vibratile membranes in the walls of the syrinx which produce the tone. The longer membranes of the larger species of course vibrate more slowly and yield lower-pitched notes."

Miller then goes on to explain that internal modifications make the above rule inoperative in the sexual size differences in owls: "These general correlations are subject to several modifying influences: 1) The enlarged syrinx, and its membranes, varies from 203 to 238 per cent of the diameter of the unmodified bronchus in males of the ten species of the *Strigidae* examined. 2) In females the enlargement is less, namely 190 to 209 per cent, and this results in shorter membranes and higher-pitched notes even though body size of females is larger than that of corresponding males." So when you hear a pair of owls, don't be swayed by logic, for the smaller males have the deeper voices while the females, though bulkier, still retain their femininity by calling a bit higher.

Plumage or coloration differences are of little value in differentiating the sex of owls. With most species, the genders are so alike that only a slight difference can be detected even in museum collections of numerous skins and then only by comparison. However, there is one glaring exception—the Snowy Owl. Fully adult individuals of this northern bird show sexual differences in the number of dark spots on the over-all white plumage. The males are almost pure white whereas the females usually have a polka-dot appearance.

PELLETS Almost every chapter of this volume reports food statistics — some of which were determined by examining the pellets of owls, those odd elliptical balls of undigested fur and bones that are to be found under owl roosts or lining their nests. Some nests — and this is especially true of Barn Owl nests that are protected from the weather — will contain thousands of these in various stages of desiccation. Fresh ones will be somewhat shiny, coated with mucus, which I assume acts as a lubricant when the pellet is regurgitated. As the pellets age they dry, and the tightly packed fur giving them their form breaks apart and reveals the skulls and other bones of animals upon which the owls have been feeding.

Most owls do not bother to tear small prey apart but instead swallow it whole with almost no injury to the bony structure of the animal eaten. After a period of many hours, from eight to sixteen, all the nutrients available in the eaten prey have been absorbed by the bird, leaving nothing but the disarticulated bony skeleton and fur or feathers in the ventriculus of the predator. This accumulation of indigestible parts takes on its pellet form about eight hours after ingestion but is sometimes retained by the bird for another six hours or so before being coughed up in the nest or below the roost.

Grim and Whitehouse summarize the procedure of pellet formation in *The Auk* (July 1963): ". . . the process of pellet formation in owls seems to occur as follows: an owl retains its animal meal within the ventriculus by closure of the sphincter between the ventriculus and proventriculus; the pyloric opening, which is small and arises superiorly, probably remains open during most of the digestive process. In this actively contracting and relaxing pouch collect enzymatic secretions arising from the glands of the proventriculus, small intestine, and pancreas. Although the general enzymatic action in digestion is little known, there is evidence that in young owls the gastric pH is distinctly acidic, becoming more neutral in older birds.

"As digestion proceeds, the nutrient effluent is pumped into the small intestine by ventricular contractions. Indigestible solids, e.g., bone, fur, teeth, nails, and chitinous materials, collect in the inferior portion of the ventriculus, and are gradually forced into a tight pellet form. The length of time between feeding and regurgitation of a pellet is subject to both internal and external factors ([D.] Chitty, 1938). In the hungry Great Horned Owl in our laboratory, pellet formation was essentially complete eight hours after feeding.

"Before regurgitation, an event [G.] Guerin (1928) held to be voluntary, the pellet lies in the superior portion of the ventriculus immediately below the sphincter. At expulsion, the sphincter is relaxed, and ventricular contraction, with accessory contractions of the abdominal wall and proventriculus, force the pellet upward in a series of steps until it is finally discharged; the process in the Great Horned Owl takes approximately four minutes."

So the next time you pick up a pellet, consider the effort expended in its formation. Don't waste it; examine it carefully and see how beneficial owls really are. Aside from some of the soft-bodied invertebrates that are completely digested, pellets are an accurate check on menus of the past. Mammalogists have also found them helpful in making comprehensive censuses of small animals occurring in a given region. The first indication that flying squirrels were resident on Mt. Palomar, California, came from the discovery of several skulls in owl pellets by Laurence Huey. At a much earlier date (1888), A. K. Fisher discovered the presence of Cooper's mice at Munson Hill, Virginia, by finding the remains of three in Long-eared Owl pellets. My detection of gopher skulls in pellets ejected by the Coronado Island Barn Owls (California) showed, after several years of search revealed no gophers on the island, that the owls had a strange extended hunting range (at least eight miles over the ocean).

ACCURACY OF STATISTICS   It has been argued that food statistics based on pellet examinations are subject to error, but that stomach examinations are always correct. From both pellet and stomach examinations I have made, I believe both are accurate, especially with regard to solid foods taken by the birds. Caterpillars and some of the other soft-bodied insects rarely show by either method. Dr. Paul Errington, quoted in A. C. Bent's account of Barred Owls, stated that ". . . in one experiment 55 English sparrows (released alive in cage) were eaten in 154 hours" by one owl; and 49 sets of mandibles were recognized n the pellets. This argues against the theory that pellets are unreliable as indicators of birds eaten. Would that all evidence

were so accurate! John and Frank Craighead, in *Hawks, Owls and Wildlife* (1956), made a conclusive study on captive birds in an effort to ascertain the accuracy of pellet statistics and ". . . determined that approximately 69 per cent of the rodents fed to a captive Marsh Hawk was evident in the pellets, whereas practically 100 per cent was found in the Short-eared Owl pellets." This variation between the two birds that live on the same foods may be explained by the greater digestive power of hawks, which habitually dissolve some bony material and also usually tear their prey apart and break or crumble bones in feeding. Owls, however, often swallow their prey almost whole and dismember it by slow internal processes.

EGGS   There are few rules that apply to all owls. Generally speaking, these birds—like all creatures—are individualists. However, they display remarkable uniformity in their eggs. The eggs have two seemingly constant characteristics—they are white and they are almost round. This matter of being white, and also round, could be a clue to their ancestral habits, now lost by some of them.

It is believed that in a very general way families of birds laying white eggs have, since their beginning, been cavity nesters. There are examples that support this point. Here in the United States it holds true with the eggs of woodpeckers and kingfishers, as well as some other bird families that nest in the darkness of hidden homes, where protective coloration and markings are not needed. Nature is not wasteful of its survival techniques. If needed, they can be developed. The generally round shape of all owl eggs, then, also seems to bolster the general theory about cavity nesters—for, as oologists have often noticed, the more precarious the nest site the more elliptically pointed the eggs of the species will be. Such egg shape reaches its peak of perfection with some of the sea birds that nest on narrow rock ledges. On each take-off and each return, the adult sea birds either jar the eggs by their clumsiness or cause them to move by the air disturbance from their wildly beating wings. But the eggs in their precarious position roll in a tight circle and return to their original position. With few exceptions it will be found that an elliptical shape is characteristic of eggs laid where rolling could endanger them. Owl eggs, however, have none of this "intelligence," being almost spherical enough to grace a pool table without detection, and this, combined with their whiteness, points a finger to the distant past when crannies, holes, or crevices were presumably the early homes of all owls.

PERMANENCE OF NESTING SITES   That some birds

occupy the same nest year after year is well known, especially when the occupants have played a part in the lives of men. Falcons, for instance, long important in the sport of falconry, are known in England to have occupied the same eyrie for over three hundred years. There are similar records in other parts of the world.

The value of owls, however, has only recently been realized, for until early in the twentieth century most of them found were shot on sight. However, there are a few outstanding records that should be mentioned, among the most notable being that of the Flushing, Long Island, Barn Owls that started me on this lifelong study. These Flushing birds were first found in the 1880's and with but a few man-caused breaks maintained their residence in that church tower until the publicity I gave them in 1927 led to the death of the last nesting pair. Thereafter the site was unoccupied. Dr. Arthur Allen knew of a Great Horned Owl nest near Ithaca that was occupied constantly for over half a century.

The cavity-nesting Screech and Elf Owls seemingly return to the same trees or cacti within which they nested in previous years. However — and this is especially true in saguaro cactus — they do not necessarily use the *identical* cavity but sometimes move to one of the many others that the Gila Woodpeckers yearly excavate in their home territory. The nesting of some species, especially the Long-eared and to a lesser extent the Short-eared, is not controlled by love of the neighborhood, for these birds have a slight tendency to colonize, and when this occurs several pairs will eliminate their food supply and will then be forced to move to more bountiful areas. There are many instances of their nesting far from their usual haunts if rodents in other areas become abundant.

JUVENILE CANNIBALISM   Most observers doing extensive

work with nestling birds of prey have encountered nests where some young have mysteriously disappeared. These disappearances have generally been blamed upon raccoons, opossums, ravens, or some other unseen predator, and if the entire brood disappears, this could be a logical assumption. However, in almost every case of infant disappearance that has occurred in my studies it has been the smallest and weakest of the offspring that has vanished, and with Barn Owls it had occurred generally during periods of rain, when the ability of the adults to catch food is not up to standard. Since all the offspring are on a starvation diet in those periods, I firmly believe that the weakest, which could be the youngest, becomes the victim of its larger brothers and sisters and possibly even its parents!

The graduated sizes of young to be found in the nests of most nocturnal predatory birds results from the fact that incubation usually starts soon after the laying of the first or second egg. The series hatching that occurs, stretching over long periods, produces a tremendous difference in the size of the young. The first to be hatched are husky and well fed; but the last, especially if there is a shortage of food, are sluggish in their development. Their only chance of survival is in a so-called rodent year, when every owl nest has its edges heaped with uneaten food. Let this surplus disappear, even for a short time, and the youngest of the nestlings will usually disappear also. Although cannibalism shocks many people, it is a logical system that maintains a seasonal balance based on available food.

SNAPPING MANDIBLES The beak-snapping of owls when disturbed is so common a characteristic that most authors list it with calls. The sound is produced in two ways, depending on the age and proficiency of the owl making the noise. Young owls clamp their upper and lower mandibles on their tongue and then suddenly draw it in. Up to the age of about three or four weeks, overly pestered Barn Owls will snap this way to the point where the tongue bleeds. As they grow older, however, they develop a less painful method, by forcing the lower mandible to or beyond the tip of the upper, and then clenching the two together. When the lower mandible is suddenly withdrawn to its normal position, the beak snaps shut with a resounding click.

FLIGHT Many owls are almost moth-like in flight, pursuing a zigzag course. Screech and Horned Owls, however, are usually direct and unwavering fliers. On take-off from a branch, both of them drop a foot or more as though to gain speed, and then with a few vigorous pumps of the wings course along above ground until they are almost beneath their chosen landing spot. Then with set wings they bank sharply upward, almost vertically, and settle gently on their perch with a minimum of wing action to retard their forward progress.

By contrast, the light, buoyant flight of Barn, Short-eared, and Long-eared Owls usually starts with a vigorous shove of the legs that launches them into the air, where elevation and speed are attained with powerful wing strokes. Their landings are also different, usually done from a horizontal plane or possibly a bit higher than the selected perch. In place of a slow-down caused by an upward zoom, which is what Screech and Horned Owls do, these three bank to a stop with flapping wings used as brakes.

Around a nest, however, the flights of the last three owls can vary considerably. As a rule all will try to leave their homes unobtrusively, and such secretiveness, especially with Barn and Long-eared, must necessitate the change from normal departures from a roost. When Long-eared Owls are first disturbed at the nest, they maneuver a dropping take-off, as though to use treetrunk, branches, or bushes as shield. But after a few human visitations to the same nest, the adults, seemingly realizing that their nest location is known to the enemy, abandon their effort to conceal their movements and resume their normal take-off pattern.

COURTSHIP DISPLAY

Although it has been stressed that most owls rely on color, form, and lack of actions to shield them from being discovered, there are a few exceptions that have been noted by the author. No doubt others will be detected in future observations. The marsh-dwelling Short-eared Owl, by flying during daylight and clapping its wings together, definitely advertises itself. However, this is a semidiurnal bird, easily observed, whereas most of the other owls during their active hours are hidden by darkness.

Observations of Horned Owls show that they complement their series of hoots when near the nest by posturing their bodies at a horizontal angle, lifting their tails to an absurd angle, and swelling the normally concealed white feathers of their throats. On one occasion, after being led by the calls, I finally detected an owl on a distant branch. At no time could I see the entire bird, but the distended white throat during the calling kept him from blending into the darkness.

TRANSPORTATION OF FOOD

Although the talons of owls are fully as capable as those of hawks in the carrying of prey, the nocturnal birds seemingly prefer to fly with feet uncluttered. In hundreds of observations made of owls of various species, I have noticed that their deliveries of food to young are usually made by

Light prey is generally carried in the beak,
as illustrated by the Screech Owl above with a moth,
while heavier prey is carried in the talons.
At right a Saw-whet carries a rat

where migrating hawks first touched the mainland after long flights from northern regions. The main prop was a sod hut, small but roomy enough for a man to remain hidden and still work strings that ran in three directions. The first of these cords tethered a shrike to a perch in such a way that a tug could pull him from sight at a moment's notice. The shrike's duty was to sight an approaching falcon when it was just a tiny spot in the sky, far too distant for human eyes to detect. As soon as this job was done he was pulled into hiding.

Simultaneously, other strings were pulled to awaken a sleepy owl, which, by means of jesses, was forced to either flap its wings or fly to another perch along a wire connecting two poles. The owl, being large and easily differentiated from other birds, was seen by the approaching hawk, whose course irresistibly veered toward it. When the distance shortened to a hundred yards or so, more strings were pulled. These ran to a pigeon tethered on the moor, forcing the bird to flap its wings, a motion that generally drew the falcon toward it as though mesmerized. As soon as talons were set in the prey, the falcon, unaware of the trap, and the pigeon were drawn to a waiting bow-net that was sprung when they both reached the right position.

The use of owls in this or some similar manner probably predates any other use of the birds by man, but in recent years the antagonism that owls arouse in hawks has been responsible for thousands of deaths of these beneficial creatures under the guise of "sport." There are many spots in the world that, like the falcon meadow of Holland, almost act as funnels for migrating birds of prey. Cape May, New Jersey; Hawk Mountain, Pennsylvania; and Assateague Island, Virginia, are a few along the Atlantic coast where owls have been used to perpetrate decimation of hawks by humans.

At Cape May, owls either alive or stuffed, then perched in trees, have decoyed over eight hundred hawks to their deaths in a single day. Their use in this manner is now prohibited in many states, but possibly making this sport illegal was not done soon enough. The disappearance of nesting Peregrines where they once existed, the alarming decrease of Bald Eagles, and the scarcity of other hawks in many areas might in part be due to this early use of owls as decoys.

OWLS ANTAGONIZE OTHER BIRDS
Harassment of owls by other birds is an accepted fact. It is indulged in by most passerines and hawks whenever an owl remains in the open. Even ducks, usually placid birds, have been

A Red-shouldered Hawk angrily attacks a stuffed Barred Owl deliberately placed near the hawk's nest. Other birds, too, tend to be deeply disturbed by the presence of an owl

known to attack owls. John G. Erickson, in *The Auk* (October 1955), writes of a Short-eared Owl: "As it dropped to the ground near a small pond, seven male Pintails . . . left the water. Swinging in a wide circle, they flew directly at the owl, which was again in the air, and forced it to swerve. This was repeated again and again for several minutes until owl and ducks disappeared behind a hill. Throughout this episode the ducks flew as a compact group . . . At this time, of course, migration was still underway and nesting of the ducks had apparently not begun." When non-nesting ducks become belligerent at sight of an owl the urge must be pretty strong.

OWLS AS FALCONS   Although owls are capable of catching much the same prey as hawks, their use—to do the bidding of man as hawks are used in falconry—has had but mediocre success. As beginning falconers, John and Frank Craighead trained Barn Owls to work from a glove and catch mice. Horned Owls, which would more appropriately be called pets than trained birds, have caught rabbits. And I have had a Screech Owl that would fly from my hand and snatch English Sparrows from an ivy-covered chimney which the sparrows used as a night roost.

Young owls, however, can be flown at what falconers term "at hack." By this system the fledglings, not yet able to fly, are placed on a shaded platform or, in the case of cavity-nesting owls, in an open-sided box. Feeding is done at a specified time each evening and great care should be taken not to scare the young into premature flight. Voluntary exercise will strengthen their wings and their first flight should not take them too far from the free meals to which they have become accustomed. They sometimes miss returning on the first night, but hunger generally brings them back on the second. As I, and others, have found out, the young usually rely on the donated food for from six weeks to two months before returning to the wild. This "hacking" of owls might, in the future, be used to restock areas where they have been foolishly eliminated before their value was recognized.

OWLS AS PETS   Generally speaking, owls make unsatisfactory pets, for although they are brilliant as far as their survival in the wild is concerned, few tame to the point of being actually friendly and those that have developed trust toward humans were removed from the nest at a very young age. Moreover, the raising of owls from infancy to adulthood is an extremely difficult and tedious process. Not many people have the skill and the patience. Complete knowledge of food habits is essential, and because of the failure to meet even minimum requirements, fully ninety percent of owls hand-raised from infancy go through life in a weakened and sometimes deformed condition. In short—don't try it. Let them remain wild and a benefit to the world.

LONGEVITY   As captives in scientifically run zoos, most owls seem to be extremely long-lived. In fact the only ones that might have a shorter life span when in captivity than in the wild are the Long-eared, Short-eared, and Great Grays. There have been so few of the latter in captivity that aviculturists have not had a chance to experiment with their care. Longevity records, however, on all animals have only recently been considered important, and many of those old records once viewed as fact are probably exaggerated. I personally cannot believe the tales of hundred-year-old parrots, for most of them are based on memory and therefore subject to the vagaries and embellishments of memory.

There seem to be some authentic records of Horned Owls that have lived at least twenty-five years. Barn Owls have been captives for at least fifteen, Elf Owls at the Arizona-Sonora Desert Museum at least seven, and Burrowing Owls up to ten. Since most zoos are now keeping systematic acquisition and death records, statistics in the distant future can be relied upon.

BREEDING IN CAPTIVITY   Captive breeding records, like those on longevity, have likewise only recently been considered important, but from experiences at the Arizona-Sonora Desert Museum and other comparable institutions there are good possibilities in the captive breeding of all species if they are given suitable care. At this Tucson "zoo-museum" a pair of Horned Owls raised young every year in an enclosure with about four other adults, and Burrowing Owls raised young over a period of five successive years.

A young boy in Tucson, Arizona, by telephone, gave a running account of a pair of local Screech Owls that he had gotten as young. One year after they were procured they began to show a proprietary interest in a nest box. Eventually young emerged from the box. Although the cage wherein this feat was accomplished was not large, about four by four by four, it was probably the diligence of their young keeper that

The second generation of young Snowy Owls bred in the Copenhagen Zoo appears to have adjusted to life in captivity

brought success. He kept about twenty-five mousetraps continuously set on the desert, as well as spending at least a half hour a day with a butterfly net catching grasshoppers and other insects to augment the owls' diet. Many other captive owl breeding records are noted in the various editions of The International Zoo Yearbook.

Burrowing Owls: There is one record from England early in the century, and two recent records for the United States, most notably that at the Arizona-Sonora Desert Museum, where young were successfully hatched and raised for several successive seasons. About seven adults occupied the cage where this captive breeding occurred, and although the actual parents would attack cage mates when the nest contained eggs or helpless young, they permitted the cage mates to feed the young soon after the fledglings emerged from their underground home. At this stage of development, however, the pair became vicious protectors of their young from any human interference, as the accompanying photo series plainly shows.

Florida Burrowing Owls: These have been successfully bred and raised to maturity at the St. Louis Zoo, and to the National Zoo, in Washington, D.C., goes the credit for the first record of the breeding and successful raising of Elf Owls.

From these breeding records of many species it seems that owls in general are almost like the cranes of the world and will reproduce in captivity if conditions are right. The possibility of breeding semi-domesticated owls might be combined with the technique of falconers who fly their young birds "at hack" until they are able to survive in the wild. If so, I believe that owls could then be reintroduced to the many regions where they have been heedlessly extirpated.

INDEX

PHOTO CREDITS

G. Ronald Austing: 40, 43,
50, 51, 57, 176–7, 191,
200, 205, 209, 230, 238,
239
Alfred M. Bailey: 210
Pete Ballestero: 227
Don Blietz: 88
Howard Cleaves: 243
F. Dufresne: 63, 68
Bruno Engler: 155, 160, 165
C. G. Hampson: 70–1, 74

Edgar T. Jones: 65
Ruth Kirk: 58
Pat Kirkpatrick and Lewis
Wayne Walker: frontis-
piece, 13, 14, 16–17, 33
Mervin W. Larson: 106, 124
Rae McIntyre: 152
Hilding Mickelsson: 77, 79,
162–3, 167, 224
Grace M. Miller: 132, 133,
136–7, 143, 147, 148, 221

O. J. Murie: 64
Erik Parbst: 246
Donald T. Ries: 203
Leonard Lee Rue III: 186
Lewis Wayne Walker: 2, 8,
24, 27, 28, 31, 35, 36, 46,
84, 87, 91, 96, 100, 101,
103, 109, 112, 115, 118,
121, 123, 128, 172, 175,
179, 181, 189, 196, 215,
216, 220, 229

A NOTE ABOUT THE TYPE

The text of this book was set in a film version of the Linotype face called Baskerville. The face is a facsimile reproduction of types cast from molds made for John Baskerville (1706–75) from his designs. The punches for the revived Linotype Baskerville were cut under the supervision of the English printer George W. Jones. John Baskerville's original face was one of the forerunners of the type style known as "modern face" to printers—a "modern" of the period A.D. 1800.

The book was composed by American Can Company—Printing Division, Clarinda, Iowa; printed by The Murray Printing Company, Forge Village, Massachusetts; bound by The Book Press, Inc., Brattle-boro, Vermont.

The book was designed by Earl Tidwell.